Advanced Praise for
To the Left of Inspiration

"Katherine Schneider tells you from ⟨...⟩ ⟨...⟩k about a blind saint or suffering survi⟨...⟩ ⟨...⟩o long ones, she says, and figures that ⟨...⟩ ⟨...⟩w many carrots she eats, no airline will be hiring her to fly their airplanes anytime soon. What is so remarkable about this book, in fact, is the incredibly credible, extraordinary ordinariness of its bright and warm and funny narrator, Dr. Katherine Schneider. In every chapter of the life as revealed in these pages—Schneider as student, as psychologist, as wife, child, sister, foster mother, or friend—the presence of intelligence, generosity, and humor sparkle. She'll make you laugh and cry, and teach you some profound lessons along the way. She's fond of lists, too, and provides some wonderful ones. My personal favorites are an A to Z list of what it feels like to be blind, and a collection of rights not written in law books (like the right to have a bad day). If you want the inside scoop on what it might really be like to be blind, read this book. You'll get to know her in these pages, and you won't so much marvel at her talents or be awestruck by her coping skills as you will just plain want to know her better, be her friend. "If I could see, I'd lose part of who I am," she writes, and when that honest pragmatism is mixed with, say, her monologue on finding the bathroom, the result is, well, just "to the left of inspiration"."

—Deborah Kendrick, award-winning columnist and author, disability rights advocate, and senior features editor for *AccessWorld*

"Respected psychologist Katherine Schneider, Senior Psychologist Emerita of the University of Wisconsin Counseling Service, who happens to be blind, has quite a story to tell. Make that stories. She offers us her arm and leads us behind the scenes through one revealing episode after another. This book should be in the curriculum of every university that educates psychotherapists and in the library of everyone interested in the human experience. Don't cheat yourself of the fascinating experience of reading this book."

—Kenneth S. Pope, PhD, ABPP, Diplomate in Clinical Psychology

To The Left Of Inspiration

Adventures in Living with Disabilities

Katherine Schneider

First published by Dog Ear Publishing
4010 W. 86th Street, Ste H
Indianapolis, IN 46268
www.dogearpublishing.net

ISBN: 1-59858-131-7
Library of Congress Control Number: 2006922272

This book is printed on acid-free paper.

Printed in the United States of America

Contents

Introduction: A Book in Search of a Title

I started writing this book in my mid-forties. Some friends asked me what I was writing about and I launched into an explanation of my project: "I am writing a humorous book about living with a disability." Usually by the time I paused for breath, these friends were leaving to alphabetize their spices or complete another pressing project.

I was born blind, and as one of the fifty-four million Americans who have a disability, I have the face validity to write on this subject. Ten years ago I developed fibromyalgia, a condition similar to chronic fatigue syndrome. As a curious person who devours books to understand new topics, I have also read widely books by and about people with various disabilities.

One of the biggest problems I faced in writing this book was choosing a title to match its spirit. This is not a "walk on water" book, as one of my friends calls books about disabilities. The only time I walk on water is during Wisconsin winters. Even then I sometimes slip. Thus, the title cannot be *Triumph Over...*, or *I Overcame...*, or anything like that. There have been moments of triumph in my life, just as there have been in everyone's, but they are few and far between.

Then there are the survivor-, sufferer-, and victim-type books. These are what Nancy Mairs, in her wonderful book, *Voice Lessons: On Becoming a (Woman) Writer*, calls "personal disaster" books. Since my life is not over, I can't say for sure whether I have survived. Sure, I have suffered; but haven't we all? So everyone could write a sufferer book. The metaphor of brokenness figures prominently in some victim-type books. I can identify with a cracked pot, but only on some days.

Humorous titles are also appealing, but the best one I know is *Splashes of Joy in the Cesspool of Life,* by Barbara Johnson. Perhaps I could get her permission to do *Daughter of Cesspool* or *Cesspool II.*

Another category of books that this book *isn't* is the "triumph over adversity" book. This is not a book that offers five steps to seeing better or tells you "you have no limits." I don't believe you can overcome everything with proper nutrition and imagery.

Then there's the issue of what to call what's "wrong" with me. Since the 1990s there has been the question of political correctness. Do I have disabilities, handicaps, or challenges? Since I was born fifty-some years ago, long before political correctness, I choose to call a spade a spade: I am blind, I have a disability. I worked in an academic setting, but I still opt for the shortest word possible to describe a situation.

If this is neither a "courageous book about a very special person" nor a "meditation enabled me to kiss my Seeing Eye™ dog goodbye" book, what is it and why should you read it? Because it is a collection of some of the pearls of wisdom I've acquired during my fifty-some years of life, and I'd like to share them with you. There are little pearls and big pearls in this collection. Chances are good that sometime in your life you, a friend, or a family member will have a chronic illness or disability. The longer you live, the better the chances get. I believe that forewarned is forearmed! Think of this as a travel book about going somewhere you don't want to go, but your job is sending you there anyway.

I began to despair of ever finding a title, when serendipity stepped in. I was in a bookstore looking for a gift for a friend and the clerk pointed me to a section "to the left of 'Inspiration'." Eureka! The perfect title! I decided to subtitle it, "Adventures in Living with Disabilities," so library catalogers will know where to put it.

If you are ready to experience the humorous but not always inspirational life, as it really is, of a blind woman, then read on!

Who am I? Growing Up with a Disability

I discovered that I was blind when I was three. I was with my brother, three years older and sighted, out in the backyard of our red brick house in Kalamazoo, Michigan. We were pulling dandelions out of the lawn. We each got a penny for every dandelion we pulled, and I was hard at work earning money for a doll I wanted. At that point in my life, I could see the yellow flowers if I was six inches above them. So I was crawling around on my hands and knees with my nose almost touching the grass. My brother, of course, was scooping them out from a much greater distance and getting a lot more. The realization hit me suddenly: he was getting more because he could see and that wasn't fair! I lay down and howled, kicking the grass with my three-year-old perspective on the unfairness of life. My parents did the right thing: nothing. Over the last thirty years as a counselor, I have worked with hundreds of people who have realized at various ages that life is not fair. The realization comes hard at any age. After I finished my fit of rage, I got back to work picking dandelions. After all, I really did want that doll. The story has a happy ending: I did eventually earn enough to purchase her. She came complete with glasses (no dolls with white canes or guide dogs were available in the early 1950s).

My parents realized much earlier than I did that I was blind. I had been born a month premature and spent a month in an incubator with high levels of oxygen. Ten years later, doctors realized that these high levels were not necessary and were shorting out the retinas of premature babies. By six months, it was obvious that I wasn't following objects with my eyes. My parents began the treks to doctors that are characteristic of the lives of parents who have children with disabilities. A University of Chicago research study on these premature infants gave my parents access to testing and guidance about how to raise a blind child. I was pronounced "above average" in intelligence and my parents were encouraged to mainstream me—integrating, as it was then called—rather than sending me to the residential school for the blind eighty miles away.

God must have known what he was doing putting me into this family. My mother had a master's degree in teaching the deaf and knew enough about mainstreaming to want it for her daughter. She worked with school authorities from the principal to the school board to establish a resource room where I could learn Braille and typing. She personally did the endless hours of reading aloud to me to make up for the books that were not available in Braille or on tape.

Teachers were also keys in the success of my mainstreaming; so much so that I can still remember the names of each of my kindergarten through twelfth-grade teachers. They did the necessary extras long before there were laws mandating accommodations. They read aloud what they wrote on the blackboards. They assigned me a chore I could do, like watering the plants instead of erasing the blackboards. They stayed after school to listen to me read my math homework aloud.

Mainstreaming worked for me by putting me into situations where I had to compete with sighted kids and cope with unequal situations. As a result, I quickly learned to ask for what I needed. When the class started playing volleyball in fourth grade, the only part of me that connected with the volleyball was my head. I learned after a few encounters of this kind to ask to be excused from the volleyball games. Unfortunately, adaptive physical education at the time wasn't an option, so I stood in the corner. My self-esteem was based on being the captain of the spelling bee team, not the volleyball team.

Mainstreaming also gave me course choices that I would not have had at a residential school, but also limited some choices that I would have had there. For example, in seventh grade, the choices were home economics (for girls; this was the early 1960s), shop (for boys), art (mainly visual), and music. I was counseled into music even though I couldn't carry a tune in a bucket. The home economics teacher had let it be known that she didn't want me in her class.

She was afraid that I would burn down the building with my attempt at cooking. Now, Public Law 94-142 would enable me to take cooking; then, I took singing (quietly, please!). But in twelfth grade, I could take pre-calculus and physics. In the lab sciences, I was allowed to do what I could (including getting frog eggs under my fingernails, just like everyone else). I concentrated on the calculations instead of performing the experiments in our lab groups. Cheerleading and being on the homecoming court were not options for me as the only blind student in my high school. Instead I joined the chess club, where the boys were.

As for cooking, I didn't learn to do that until I was a graduate student living in my own apartment. My mother also worried about me possibly burning down the house with my cooking efforts. Just to set the record straight: in over thirty-five years of daily cooking, I have had one fire. It set my flannel shirt on fire and I thoroughly singed myself, but did nothing to the house. Swaddled in bandages, I cooked the next day to make sure I still could.

In seventh grade, I began to learn to use a long cane. I got around in school by memorizing what was where. At first I hated the cane! It marked me as different and blind. Growing up in sighted society, I had the usual stereotypes of blind people. They fumbled around and couldn't do much. The only blind people in our readers in those days were Louis Braille, the inventor of the writing system for the blind, and Helen Keller, who was also deaf. These, and one wretched poem about seven blind men going to see an elephant, were the only times people like me were mentioned. No wonder I didn't want to carry a cane and be publicly labeled as "blind"! Of course, walking very slowly around school carrying a Braillewriter and a stack of Braille books labeled me anyway, but that cane was the last straw for my fragile teenage ego. However, the teachers and student teachers from Western Michigan University's Orientation Mobility program were smart. They capitalized on what every teen wants almost as much as fitting in: independence. They asked, "Do you want to be able to go downtown alone? Go off to college somewhere?" I could practically hear the car keys jingling! "Yes!" I replied, and kept learning to tap the cane to the left when my right foot went forward.

When it was time for college, even though there were four

colleges in Kalamazoo, I knew I had to leave my protective home setting and test my independence. So I went to Michigan State University, a school of 42,000. It was eighty-six miles away from home (the limit my parents had given me was ninety miles). For the first time in my life, I wasn't Katherine Schneider, the first blind student in the Kalamazoo Public Schools. I was just another student, and I loved it! There were about twenty other blind students at Michigan State, and we met as we passed in the reading rooms set aside for reading aloud in the library. At first, I assiduously avoided the rest. They were blind. What could I possibly have in common with such low-lifes? Later I made some good friends among them and began to realize that some blind people I like, and some I don't. We are people first, after all!

I started out majoring in physics, a career aspiration of mine since seventh grade. But after two tries at a particular calculus class and a C- in advanced chemistry, I began to wonder. Could I not hack it because I was blind, as many suggested? Or was it because my brain just didn't work in that way? At the same time, I needed a class at 8 am. So I took psychology, and loved it! I got involved with crisis phones and other volunteer work where my listening skills, honed for twenty years as a matter of survival, came in handy. I was off and running toward a career in clinical psychology. A PhD from Purdue University (what else could an overachiever do but go for a PhD?), teaching and counseling, and administrative work at counseling centers at universities in four states have given me thirty full years of a professional life.

But before you assume, gentle reader, that "she lived happily ever after" and that this is one of those "walk on water books," despite what I said in the preface, read on! In living this life, I have had many opportunities to rise and fall, but also to rise and limp onward.

What Does it Feel like to be Blind?

Blindness brings with it a wealth of feelings. Just like the ABCs, my feelings can range from A to Z. On any given day, I might experience any or all of the feelings I've listed below.

Anger: I am angry when discrimination occurs; for example, when I go to vote and I have to take someone into the voting booth with me. No secret ballot for me!

Boredom: If I can't take enough reading material on vacation and can't read what's available at newsstands, I get bored.

Confusion: When someone is describing an intersection and says it is shaped like a cloverleaf, I wonder: what *does* that look like?

Disappointment: I'm disappointed when a student who is scheduled to read to me does not show up.

Exasperation: Exasperation happens when I've explained my needs, like keeping cabinet doors closed, but people still leave them half open.

Frustration: I get frustrated, especially when several of the above have happened before noon!

Gray: Blindness is like a gray, cloudy day; not black and scary.

Happiness: I am happy when a client takes a positive step in therapy and says it's because we talked.

Inspiration: Reading about someone overcoming great odds inspires me.

Joy: When I make a strike in bowling, joy abounds. My Seeing Eye dog even stands up!

Kindness: I feel kindly when I meet a new Leader Dog™ pup in training. I know what big responsibilities that pup will grow into.

Laughter: Laughter erupts when I do something silly, like almost taking the dog's vitamins instead of mine before I drink my first cup of coffee in the morning.

Mystification: Why are some things appealing to sighted people—like the color chartreuse?

Nervousness: I get nervous when someone's staring at me, because I can feel it.

Outsider: During discussions about movies, I feel like an outsider when people start discussing the leading actor.

Pride: When my dog and I prance off to work in a snowstorm and arrive before sighted colleagues, we're a proud team.

Question: I have many questions, such as: will equal opportunity ever become reality?

Rapture: Oh, the rapture of a movie with descriptive video so I really know what's going on.

Self-pity: I feel self-pity when I receive a handwritten love letter and it will be three days before someone can read it to me.

Timidity: I feel timid when dealing with new situations. It takes time to educate people so they feel comfortable with me.

Uncertainty: I feel uncertain when a familiar route is impassable because of construction and I want to get home quickly in a thunderstorm.

Vulnerability: I feel vulnerable when it's twenty-five degrees below zero and I know one wrong turn and I'll be lost.

Weariness: I become weary of continuously fighting the good fight to end discrimination.

X-ray vision (not!): A neighbor thought I had X-ray vision and could see through her walls. I'm not making this up!

Yearning: At times I yearn to see, especially when I meet my new Seeing Eye dog.

Zest: I'm zestful for the next adventure!

While reading this list, if you thought to yourself, "I've felt that also," then you get the point. Whether sighted or blind, we all feel the same emotions, from anger to zest.

The Working World: Before and After the Americans with Disabilities Act of 1990

True enough, work is a four-letter word, and although those of us who have jobs grouse that we can't wait until quitting time on Friday, in this era of downsizing we are glad to be employed. This is even truer for those of us with significant disabilities, two-thirds of whom are unemployed. "Hire the Handicapped" campaigns emphasize our low rates of absenteeism and our gratitude to be employed. Clearly we have yet to reach the land of equal opportunity in the working world.

My first foray into the world of paid employment was as a dishwasher at my dorm cafeteria at Michigan State. It was a great job, with an opportunity to turn off my brain, play in the muck, and get paid for it. The staff had not worked with a blind employee before and we made up the accommodations as we went along. We agreed on some common-sense changes: my time card was kept in a particular spot, and I either scraped dishes or loaded them into the machine. It worked out well. As I look back on the experience from the vantage point of middle age, I wonder how the permanent staff, middle-aged themselves, tolerated the music and the goofing around of student workers year after year.

I started doing volunteer work at a variety of community mental health facilities and crisis centers after my freshman year of college, and discovered that psychology was the career for me. When I first started, I wondered what I would do if someone jumped me and I couldn't see them coming. In the late 1960s and early 1970s, employees were not typically trained in how to respond to violence on the job. All of us wondered what we'd do if attacked, but luckily we never had to find out. I did come close once, though. I remember a person coming into a crisis center at about two in the morning talking about the knife he had, and how he was going to use it on someone. I asked to see it, and sure enough, he did have a handsome knife. I put it on the table between us and we talked until he became less agitated. Later—hindsight is always great—I realized I should have offered to keep it for him. Throughout my career, I have been stalked and threatened a few times, but my Seeing Eye dogs have always intervened in helpful ways.

In graduate school, I was allowed to do more interviewing and less psychological testing (which depends heavily on vision). I also continued to do volunteer work at crisis centers. Answering crisis phones came naturally to me because I was accustomed to not having visual cues in conversations. In fact, when I helped train volunteers in this work, I would sometimes wonder why they were having so much trouble listening. Then they would comment on how hard it was to not be able to see the caller.

During the last year of my graduate program, I had an internship at Central Louisiana State Hospital. There I began to realize the benefits of having a Seeing Eye dog with me to communicate with patients who didn't want to talk to me. Disturbed adolescents who didn't want to talk to adults would confide in my dog, Cindy, and I could listen in if I wanted to. People who were considered "out of it" by staff members were quite kind to her. As one paranoid patient said to a bossy staff member who was ordering her not to step on the dog, "I'm crazy but not stupid!" I finished my internship with a PhD and confidence that I was going to get a terrific job and set the world on fire.

Then reality set in. I had sent out about 150 résumés for openings advertised in professional magazines. Part of my problem was my own naiveté: I sent along a letter saying I was blind, which described what I could and couldn't do. The main thing I couldn't do was drive a car, which was necessary for some rural mental health work. I received many replies saying, "You're wonderful, and we admire you, but we can't hire a blind person." One letter even went so far as to say, "We have one blind psychologist; we can't have two."

Did they think our guide dogs would fight? The moral of the story became clear to me: don't mention disabilities until an interview is granted. Then you can deal with questions and stereotypes face to face.

When I finally did get a few interviews, there were plenty of questions, both reasonable and off the wall. My favorite question was, "What would you do if someone shot up heroin in class?" I asked the interviewer, stalling for time, if that was common at his university. He said that it wasn't, but insisted on knowing what I would do if that situation arose. I said that I assumed other students would have a reaction, and I would be able to pick up on their reactions and work the crowd to help settle the problem. Thankfully, the closest I ever came to disaster in a classroom was when students cheated on exams, even though I had a sighted proctor. However, word got out that my Seeing Eye dog would sit in front of a cheater to point them out. I don't know if it was true, but I didn't do anything to squash the rumor.

I was lucky enough to land a job immediately after completing my internship. Six months of sending out resumes paid off. Another blind psychologist I knew took over a year to become employed. I had expected psychologists and counselors to be nondiscriminatory and well informed about the abilities and needs of people with disabilities, but this simply wasn't true. In every state where I have taken licensing exams, an oral exam is given to make sure the psychologist is not drunk, stoned, or noticeably crazy. However, my oral exams have focused on asking whether I read journals or how I became blind. If I hadn't kept up with the literature, how could I have passed their exam? And how is the cause of my blindness relevant to the practice of psychology? Of course, I wanted that license to hang on my wall, so I just answered the questions sweetly.

After over thirty years of seeking employment and conducting hiring searches, I would give the following advice to job seekers with disabilities: if your disability and needs are not mentioned in the interview, bring them up yourself. Be ready to tell the employer what you need. If you don't, they will rely on their own ideas, which are likely to be a lot worse than reality. Answer illegal questions minimally, but politely, and then reorient the conversation to either your strengths or questions for the employer. I don't think you'll get a job by telling someone their question is illegal!

There was one phone interview I'll never forget. Appalachian State University had reviewed my application and invited me in for an interview for an Assistant Director position at their counseling center. Then one of my references said something about how I cope with my disability, so they found out I was blind. I would have told them anyway by saying, "You'll recognize me at the airport because of my Seeing Eye dog." The phone conversation went as follows:

"We're glad you're coming for the interview."

"So am I."

"But did you know there are mountains here?"

"Yes, I live near the Poconos and it's nice to be able to visit them occasionally, isn't it?"

"We're glad you're coming, but did you know the price of land is high here?"

"That's too bad. That must be a problem for everyone."

"We're sure glad you're coming, but did you know there's snow here in the winter?"

"My crazy Labrador guide dog loves winter and bounding through snow drifts."

Finally, "We're glad you're coming, but did you know there's wind here?"

"Well, I used to live in Iowa, and we swore the wind blew straight from the North Pole."

I still haven't figured out what wind had to do with anything! Obviously, the person making this call had mixed feelings about my employment there. Luckily, I had another job offer and didn't even interview there. If I had gone there, I would have faced the challenge of convincing at least one person that blind people are not hothouse plants that need protection from wind and snow. Sadly, this person had a doctorate and was still that ignorant. It's also scary to think about him advising students with disabilities. I can laugh about it now, but what if that had been the only job prospect I'd had?

With the passage of the Americans with Disabilities Act (ADA) in 1990, discrimination in hiring became illegal. Obviously, the phone conversation I'd had was discriminatory, but it would have been my word against his in court. If I was interviewed, but not hired, how could I prove I had not been hired simply because of my dis-

ability? Apparently, the ADA has had little impact on hiring prac-
tices, probably because people with disabilities are reluctant to sue.
It's too hard to prove what was said in conversations, and even harder
to prove that their disabilities were the only reason for not being
hired.

I believe that most discrimination is based on discomfort and
a lack of knowledge, rather than meanness. So I take a more understanding approach and adopt a "Let me help you to feel comfortable
so you can do the right thing" attitude in talking to potential employers. I have also educated search committees I've been a part of about
what questions to ask and how to ask them so that the interview is not
only legal, but also fair for all kinds of people.

However, once I've been hired and my foot is in the door, then
it becomes a matter of getting what I need, contributing what I can,
and enjoying the people around me. At each workplace, some people
have gone out of their way to make me feel welcome, either by keeping treats in their desk for my Seeing Eye dog, or by describing
what's for sale in the Current© catalog that circulates around almost
every worksite where three or more women work. These little acts of
kindness go a long way towards buffering the occasional ugly and
overt acts of discrimination.

After teaching and counseling at universities for over ten
years, I decided to try working in administration. Four years in management were enough to convince me that, although I loved parts of
it, it wasn't for me. Some of this decision was due to tensions felt by
many middle managers, myself included. Did I have the power to
meet my responsibilities? And how much of a difference could I
really make? Another factor in the decision was also the isolation I
experienced from being one of a kind. At conferences for directors of
counseling centers, there were other directors who were women, and
people who remembered occasional directors with physical disabilities, but I found no mentors there. Sociologists write books about
role conflict and role strain. I was clearly living with these problems.
I wanted to find someone to have a cup of coffee with who knew
what it was like to make personnel decisions about somebody one
minute, and ask them to read me a memo the next.

Because of my blindness, both supervising and administering
have presented unique challenges. I have been in charge of someone

and at the same time depending on them to do things differently because of my blindness. Many people have risen to the occasion. Some colleagues have seen it as an opportunity to view the world differently. On the other hand, some have used it as an opportunity to behave poorly. They would make faces as I was running a meeting, or choose not to speak. I wouldn't know they were doing this, but others would see them. These situations remind me of babysitting my young nephews, who hoped they could get away with writing on the wall in lipstick because I couldn't see it. As a survey conducted by www.esight.org pointed out, managers with disabilities often face both disrespectful and resentful employees. I never figured out which management theory offered the best way to take care of this passive-aggressive behavior. In the end, I decided to go back to more counseling and less administration.

So I got back in the trenches, counseling full time, teaching occasionally, writing, and speaking. In counseling, the fact that I can't see has advantages and, occasionally, disadvantages. One advantage is that people who feel ugly (unfortunately, this is not rare) know I'm not judging their looks. Clients can tell that I've struggled and therefore may have empathy for their struggles. On the other hand, one disadvantage is that it's difficult working with very young children who don't talk much, or people with very low English skills. However, there are ways I get around these obstacles. For example, if they are international students, I encourage them to bring a dictionary to our meetings. Or if I'm not sure whether a client has a cold or is crying, I ask. Occasionally there are clients who feel they are receiving inferior counseling because I can't see. A quick transfer to a sighted colleague solves that problem.

Sometimes stereotypes are broken on both sides and we all grow. One day, I was interviewing a young Vietnamese man, and as we walked into the office I said something about the dog (as I usually do). He told me that in his country, dogs are considered food at best. I assured him that my dog would lie in the corner and not bother him, which she did. By the end of the hour, it was clear that he needed to come back for another session. I began to talk about transferring him to a different counselor so that he did not have to put up with the dog. But he said that he still wanted to see me. I said that he was very kind, but since I had the dog at every session, I wondered if he'd be more comfortable with a different counselor. He again stated he wanted to see me. I agreed that I had enjoyed talking with him and would be glad to see him again, but I wondered why he was so adamant about seeing me. He told me that in his flight from his home country, he had been tortured by being stared at, and at least I did not stare at him.

Another group of clients who often have reactions to my blindness are people with eating disorders. Some can't tolerate a counselor who is visibly imperfect. Others are comforted by knowing that I won't be seeing them as fat (which they think they are). I can also get away with asking clients to describe themselves to me. They say that they do this quite honestly because they know I can't tell. Some have even said, "I wish everybody was like you."

Having a Seeing Eye dog in sessions adds another perspective. Usually the dog greets each client, gives him or her some non-judgmental warmth, and then lies in the corner. Sometimes a student and a dog form a bond, and will stay and comfort the client when he or she is upset. I remember one situation when the dog gave some amazing nonverbal feedback. The client was whining about life not being fair, and I was trying to figure out how to kindly point out that the whining wasn't productive. My guide dog got up, walked as far away from the client as possible, lay down, and groaned. The client asked, "Why did she do that?" I suggested that the client ask the dog, but the client didn't want to hear the feedback.

One of my guide dogs was very averse to couples fighting when I first got him. I had to work with him in order to help him understand that their voices were not raised at him and that it was all right for couples to fight in my office so that they didn't fight as much at home. The dog would chase his tail to get them to stop fighting, and they'd start laughing at him. The couple would then be reminded of how their children might feel when they fight at home.

Some students with disabilities prefer to see me, the only counselor with a visible disability on campus, but others don't. It seems to depend on how ashamed they are of their own disabilities. One young woman with an artificial leg and an eating disorder became angry enough to transfer to a different counselor because she felt I was too open about my disability, and expected her to be equally open. She wanted to hide her disability, and not have to deal with it.

I was torn because I felt I was in a unique position to both support and challenge her, but I ended up supporting her decision to transfer. She was making a stand, and I wanted to empower her to do that.

Both my blindness and fibromyalgia give me many points of contact with clients who struggle daily because they can't do it all, and because they feel looked down upon by society. International students seem to realize that in many ways I'm also in a strange culture all the time, living in a world where most people have no disabilities.

Sometimes the fact that I can't see provides a good laugh in a counseling situation. One day, I was talking with a young man who was very shy. He was talking about wanting to date, but being too shy to do it. We talked and brainstormed ideas. Suddenly, he was seized by an itch in a place one can't scratch in public. He assumed that because I couldn't see him, he could relieve his itch, and I'd never know. I had to bite my lip so that I wouldn't laugh. I'm sure he would've fled if I'd let on that my well-trained hearing was able to localize that scratching sound.

Another enjoyable part of my career in psychology is being a guest lecturer and presenting workshops on mental health topics. This has taken me to a variety of community groups, such as women offenders, divorced and widowed people, and senior citizens. I get a kick out of being able to share ideas from the field of psychology with people who would not otherwise have the opportunity to see a psychologist one on one. This is probably why I also enjoy writing occasional articles for a Braille women's magazine as well as the local newspaper. I have even run a call-in radio show on a university radio station. I may not be Dr. Laura, but Dr. Kathie enjoys sharing information that might make people feel better.

I've also designed and run a mentoring program for the American Psychological Association, matching psychologists and psychology students who have similar disabilities. The mentors who volunteered have disabilities such as quadriplegia, epilepsy, blindness, and chronic fatigue. The psychologists were excited about giving back to the field by helping the next generation surmount obstacles and join their profession.

Throughout my career, I have taught classes from introductory psychology to graduate classes in counseling. One difference in my classroom is that students do not have to raise their hands, but must wait until I pause before they speak up. They report that this takes some getting used to. I also try extra hard to use videos, guest lecturers, and interactive activities so there is visual stimulation in addition to auditory. Recently I've used email journals and had students submit their papers electronically so I can grade them myself. I regret that I can't spot and greet students on campus, but electronic contact lets students know that I do take an individual interest in them. My favorite students are the ones who struggle, whether it's because they haven't been in school for many years, because they have a learning disability, or because they're not initially interested. I like the challenge of trying to make psychology make sense to these diverse students.

The thing I love most about my work is that it's never dull. No two people are alike, and even if they have the same problem, their strengths and needs are different. This has kept me both employed and fascinated for over thirty years.

My career in psychology reminds me of the Tehabi story. If you haven't met this Native American Kachina doll, let me introduce you: it's pictured as a blind man carrying a mobility-impaired man. The message of Tehabi is, "I'll see for you; you carry me." I have had a great education and counseling career, and I've been able to pass along some of what Tehabi means to students, clients, and supervisees. Tehabi lives!

A Day in the Life of Katherine Schneider

October 26, 1999

7:00 am: I got on my computer at home and reviewed thirty messages from my various electronic discussion lists dedicated to clinical psychologists, training directors, equal access to software, information for the blind and disabled, and psychology of women, as well as a list of Wisconsin Public Radio programs for the day. Next, I surfed the *New York Times, Christian Science Monitor,* and *Reuters Health* websites to see if I could find any tidbits to forward to trainees at the Counseling Center. Then I went to the Student Counseling Center's website to look for information for one of the interns doing a presentation on recognizing a relationship heading for trouble.

8:00 am: I supervised a doctoral intern my first hour at work. First, we focused on what she'd learned about teaching from being my teaching assistant yesterday. Then, we discussed what worked and what didn't work in the Psychology of Women class, particularly how I'd tried to involve the four males. We also talked about her career direction, and the setting she would most prefer after her graduation next summer. Finally, we discussed a case focusing on how to invite clients to return, both respecting their independence and letting them know that they are welcome.

9:00 am: We spent the first forty-five minutes of this week's staff meeting with the Affirmative Action officer discussing how our offices can work better together. Office business got about ten minutes of discussion time.

10:00 am: I talked with a client about a long relationship that had ended a month ago. We talked about the grieving process and letting go. Her homework was to watch herself for how often she care-takes for others by giving them unrequited advice, etc. We went out to set the next appointment and made one for thirteen days from now. Even though she would have preferred something within a week, I didn't have any times to offer. The session ended at 10:45 and I and word-processed three case notes before the next appointment.

11:00 am: I met with a long-term client struggling with control, perfectionism, and depression issues. She wanted to know what I would feel and do if she did not follow through on a medical appointment she needed. I tried to communicate that I would be disappointed but would still respect and work with her.

12:00 pm: I returned two phone calls: one to a former practicum student wanting to list me as a reference, the other to a movie producer. I asked his permission to show his video in my Psychology of Women class next Monday.

12:15 pm: I walked home, noticing what a fine day it was and enjoying the sounds of students lolling on the mall. One student was playing a guitar. I had my usual Tuesday lunch with a friend who has Alzheimer's. Our discussion focused on food and my Seeing Eye dog, Carter—both topics we enjoy discussing. Carter and the friend had a short ball game; they each let the other win occasionally.

1:15 pm: I scanned sixty emails at home, including one with the University Senate's agenda and handouts for the afternoon's meeting.

2:00 pm: I sent a no-show letter to a client that did not show up for his 2:00 appointment. I had his prior written permission, so I tried to call his hall director, but the hall director wasn't in. I returned a professor's call and arranged to guest lecture two of his classes in November. I caught up on client notes from the morning, and I gave a bit of thought to what I wanted to say at 4:00 on a panel for pre-nursing majors denied admission to the School of Nursing.

3:00 pm: I attended the University Senate meeting, which to my surprise, I am really enjoying. It's great to get updates about what's going on in different areas of the university.

4:00 pm: I talked to the pre-nursing students about how counseling could help them deal with their reactions to being denied admission to the program. I told them counseling can help them deal with depression, family problems, etc. that may get in the way of academic success.

5:15 pm: I went back to the office to return calls and to skim another thirty emails. I called a physician who is seeing one of my clients, and a person who is driving me next week to and from a presentation to first graders about disability awareness. Then, I went home for a walk and dinner.

7:00 pm: I read emails and typed up this log. I finished by 8:00, watched the Public Television series on Africa, and spent some "quality time" with Carter. After a little reading and a few prayers, I called it a day.

Social Life: Friends and Family

Family, friends, and lovers: without these the world would be so much poorer. I could show you snapshots, but in the spirit of fairness, I'll describe them instead, as I experience them.

My mother was a sensitive, intelligent, and artistic woman who stayed at home raising children in the 1950s and 1960s instead of pursuing her career in special education of the deaf. She helped with our homework, led the Girl Scout troop, and often told my brother and me what she had given up for us. After I was in high school, she began taking painting classes at the local art center and enjoyed them greatly. Health problems, exacerbated by alcoholism, led to her death at the age of seventy-five, leaving much traveling and painting undone. She turned her grief at having a blind child into pushing for me to have access to public education at a time when this wasn't common and for me to succeed at the A-plus level. If I had a snapshot of her to show you, it would be of her lying on the living room couch with a book in one hand and a cigarette in the other, reading aloud to me. Her intuitive reading of people and her love of good literature are two of her gifts to me. Her paintings hang on my living room walls, beautiful for others to see and a bittersweet reminder to me of the gap between us that loomed so large for both of us.

My father was a tall, handsome man. Even though he had the leisure and money to travel extensively in his retirement, the marks of growing up during the Depression were still visible. He shopped extensively for the best buy in a flannel shirt and he hesitated to make long-distance phone calls, especially during the expensive times. Dad had a quick and inquiring mind. As a child I remember him bringing home a briefcase full of journals to scan each night after dinner. When I lug a stack of books to school to peruse with a human reader or take them home to skim on my talking computer reading machine, I'm following in his footsteps. His discomfort with my blindness and with emotions in general extended to anything nonscientific. He liked riding steam trains, preferably in a jungle.

My brother is a bright, intense electrical engineer who inherited Dad's scientific mind and Mom's night-owl tendencies. Snapshots of him would show him at his computer at work or at home in his basement working on his model railroad. Since he and I are on opposite ends of the political spectrum, being able to talk about the Internet has been a wonderful bond for us. As we grew up, my brother got part of his allowance for walking me to school, but I wonder if some of his discontents in life go back to feeling neglected during childhood because my mother spent so much time accommodating my educational needs. Because of the conflicts between my parents, my brother and I did cling together in childhood and spent many hours playing endless games of Hearts.

When I went to college and learned both in class and from friends how dysfunctional my family was, I spent a good bit of time in therapy working through the effects alcoholism, abuse, and my parents' stormy marriage had had on me. The farther away in time and in space I got from home, the more able I became to acknowledge the positives in my childhood. I am grateful for my mainstreamed education, the "you can succeed" attitude, and the strong work ethic my parents gave to me. Accepting myself as a person with strengths and limitations, only some of them physical, has made me much more accepting of my parents as fallible human beings who did their best.

Some of the best family memories I have are of trips around the United States, Europe, and Japan. The sounds and smells of other cultures in my early years have given me empathy for international students as they try to absorb a new culture and do college work in a foreign language. My collections of little animal figurines and models of such buildings as the Eiffel Tower give me tactile knowledge of the icons of other countries.

Forming friendships wasn't natural for me, coming from a

family who stressed being independent. I remember a couple of girls in elementary school who tried to be my friends by doing things for me. My first real friend was in high school. She and I did all sorts of wild things together, like hanging out at the local bowling alley and talking our way into getting a tour of the county jail. As a joke, we took part in a study of people who had had contact with extraterrestrials. All of this was good training, I'm sure, for my friend's career as a minister and mine as a psychologist. In our friendship, it did not seem to matter that I took her arm when we walked. Perhaps this was because she had helped out in her father's hearing aid business and was used to people's special needs.

In junior high I discovered that the opposite sex was worthy of note. As the only girl in the chess club in both junior and senior high school, I had ready access to some of the species. Of course, these young men were more interested in chess than in dating, but that was okay with me. My first date was a friend's older brother who was a university student. We went to a college dance, but both of us would have preferred to have stayed home and played chess. With a special chess set, I was on a level playing field and enjoyed some envy from other girls who would have liked to spend time on a regular basis with so many males.

In college, I had a small circle of female friends with whom I discussed earth-shaking ideas, played Pinochle, and drank an occasional sloe gin fizz. I remember going to one house party where a male who was showing some interest in me was so drunk he couldn't believe I was blind, not blind drunk, until I opened my Braille watch to prove it. As a freshman, I went to a drive-in with a young man to watch the movie...I thought. I became less naïve with time.

In graduate school, I met and subsequently married a fellow student. Eventually our cultural expectations split us apart. He expected a wife who did the housework and had children. I expected that whoever got home from class first fixed dinner. It irked me that many people, from complete strangers to simple acquaintances, would say that they admired him for marrying and taking care of me when I knew the reality was quite different. I also did not like being asked immediately, when people found out I was married, whether he was blind too. He wasn't, but he was Oriental. My more liberated friends asked about our sex life. Sexual attractiveness is a whole package of sensations. Apparently many sighted people concentrate on the visual to the exclusion of all the other wonderful senses. In one word, our sex life was fine even with the lights turned out.

After the divorce, I stayed away from even male friendships for a while, to lick my wounds and figure out what had gone wrong. As a middle-aged single person now, many of my friends are other single women. Others are couples, some with children. I enjoy the diversity of having friends to talk animals with, friends to play Scrabble with, and friends to walk with. I joke that if I ever remarried it would have to be to a long-distance trucker, but the truth is that I highly value time alone.

In each friendship, especially at the beginning, we have to work out what will be different because I do not see. Will the friends pick me up if we're dining out together and will I occasionally offer to fill their gas tank? Will the friend tell me if something in my house looks unsightly? One of my friends recently realized she felt responsible not just for telling me, but also for fixing the situation and she was beginning to resent that. We agreed it would be much better for both of us if she could just tell me, and I would be in charge of doing something about it. Early on, I think I bought friendship by counseling people, or at least being their one-sided listener. As I've grown to know I'm an okay person, I do not pursue that kind of lopsided friendship and hence have more time for the give and take of more equal friendships. Young people with disabilities have often told me they struggle a lot with loneliness. There's good news ahead for them. In adulthood there are deep and wonderful friendships that do not rely on looking perfect or being on the football team.

Public Speaking, or "Can You Sing?"

Over the last thirty years, I've given at least a thousand speeches about disability awareness to groups ranging from preschoolers to senior citizens. The content of my talks has not changed much, but what keeps me giving them are people's questions and reactions.

Often for school groups I use the paperback book, titled *Different and Alike,* as my theme. The message is that I'm similar to most people in what I need and want in life, but I may accomplish my goals slightly differently. I give numerous examples, including how I read, grocery shop, tell time, and match colors, among other things.

The settings of my talks vary from posh restaurants to school basement gymnasiums. One of the gyms was memorable because a bat was swooping back and forth while I was talking. The Girl Scout leaders kept announcing to the girls, "We won't panic!" in suspiciously high-pitched voices.

As any professional speaker will tell you, the most common meal for the luncheon circuit involves some kind of baked chicken. Since I'm a vegetarian, disposing of this gracefully can be tricky. Announcing vegetarian status is not the solution. Usually that gets you a double lettuce salad—ugh!

Ninety-nine percent of the time, my Seeing Eye dog lays calmly at my feet. Then there was the time I gave a talk on stress management to a civic group. We ate lunch and made table talk. I thought to myself that this must be a really health-conscious group—damn it, no dessert! As I got up to speak, Sugar lunged and scored my cherry crisp, which had been lurking at the edge of the table. One cherry eluded her, so we stood rooted to the spot until she cleaned that up, too. I muttered something to Sugar about killing her later, but she smacked her lips and said she'd die happy anyway. The audience was laughing so hard seeing my "kid" screw up in public that I really didn't have to say much about the benefits of humor in stress management. We got voted best program of the year.

Adults' questions are not that much different from kids'. They range from "How do you get food into your mouth?" to "If two Seeing Eye dogs have babies, will their pups be Seeing Eye dogs?" Usually after I speak, I get enough compliments to send me home needing a bigger hat. One time, however, two men stood in the back of the room quite audibly discussing whether to give me a dollar or not. They decided that I wasn't worth it. I wondered if they'd been dozing when I'd said, "Don't pity us" and "Blind people can usually hear." Another time a lady came up afterwards to ask me to sing for them. Apparently her stereotype that all blind people are musical was still intact. I let her down gently by telling her that I only sing in the shower, and that when I sing the dog will leave the room if she can.

Often parents and grandparents want to know how to teach their children about disabilities. I tell them it's okay for kids to notice and comment on differences. Instead of saying, "shh," I'd prefer that a parent explain, "Yes, she's blind and that dog sees for her."

In public speaking situations, the unexpected happens just often enough to keep me on my toes. After one nursing home talk I was told, "You're okay, but I preferred the man with a tiger last month."

Another area of public speaking that I've dabbled in is making television appearances. Apparently this wasn't a favorite occupation for my Seeing Eye dog, Cindy. As we three mental health experts sat around a coffee table discussing some pressing mental health issue, she lay dutifully under the table. Then she began to flatulate. The talk proceeded and so did the gas. Three mental health experts kept smiling professionally while wanting to say "phew" and throw open the nearest door. Uncharitable folk might say that the dog wasn't producing any more gas than the three mental health experts.

When I took a lay-speaking class from a Methodist church in Arkansas, they taught us that a good way to prepare a sermon was to have three points, a poem, and a prayer. They also endorsed the KISS method: (keep it short, stupid). This has been a good counterpoint for me to the academic, fifty-minute-lecture approach.

Basically, what I want people to remember is: offer help, ask the questions you need to, and enjoy the differences we have as well as the similarities we share. Lately, I think some people have become afraid to notice the difference, thinking it is not politically correct to do so. If you are busy pretending that I see and I really don't, we have a big barrier. A friend said recently, "I almost asked you what so and so looked like but I caught myself." When we can laugh together about our different perspectives, I've accomplished the goal of my public speaking: breaking down barriers and minimizing stereotypes.

Travel Light, But Don't Forget the Dog Food

I love to travel. I've lived in seven states, and every year I have traveled at least once to professional meetings and a couple of times to visit out-of-state relatives and friends. Four of my six dogs have been with me to both coasts, so I think I qualify as a veteran traveler. Anyone who travels frequently knows why comedians get some of their best laughs from stories about airports, luggage, and travel woes. But since I am not awake late enough to go on the late night talk shows with my stories, I'll share the best of them with you now. If you're reading this book in an airport, I suggest you switch to a different chapter.

Travel is wonderful, but scary for many—hence the numerous bars in even medium-sized airports. In addition to the usual concerns about luggage, flights, connections, and food, I have concerns about timely assistance and dog-pottying needs. The good news is I've somehow always gotten where I needed to go. Every time I travel, I get the opportunity to be reminded how good-hearted and helpful most people are. Whether it's airline personnel helping me between flights or a fellow bus rider holding my dog's leash while I use the bus toilet (barely big enough for a human behind, let alone a human plus a Seeing Eye dog), I have often been helped by strangers who have nothing to gain.

Once while traveling to a meeting in Houston, I was chatting on the plane with a man who lived there. When we exited the plane, I asked him to help me find ground transportation; instead, he offered to take me to my hotel. Twenty minutes later, when we were out on the freeways of Houston, it suddenly dawned on me that if this wasn't a nice person I could be in the ditch with my throat slit, and no one would miss me for several days. But he was a nice man, and there have been so many folks that have gone out of their way to help just as he did.

Have you ever been bored in a bus terminal, railroad station, or airport? I rarely am. I used to carry lots of Braille reading matter, but now I carry little and do a lot of people watching instead. A Seeing Eye dog draws the people to me like a magnet. First come the children, bored and antsy, who spot a dog they hope to pet. Next come the parents, hoping to retrieve a child with all of their fingers still intact. Then come the dog lovers, and the people connected with Lions Clubs, which sponsor some guide dog schools. Finally, the just plain bored who have already exhausted the newsstands and coffee shops arrive. If we are waiting out some kind of delay, a passenger's grapevine of information often develops after the ice breaking chat about the dog.

During these delays, I have become aware of a feature of airports' accessibility that I don't think is in airport planning manuals yet: how quickly a person can find a place for a guide dog to relieve itself. Somewhere between six and eight hours after the last comfort stop, this becomes a pressing question. In the over thirty-five years I have traveled with guide dogs, I can remember three incidents when we didn't quite make it. The most memorable time occurred after I visited my brother and his family and was joining my parents for a vacation in Michigan. My dog had enjoyed a lot of attention from my young nephews, and had eaten a few too many grapes. (For those offended by bathroom humor, or who have never had a bit too much of the grape in one form or another, please skip the next paragraph.)

My parents and I were proceeding down one of the main concourses of the O'Hare terminal. My mother was in a wheelchair, pushed alternately by my father and an airline person, with my Seeing Eye dog and me trotting along behind. The grapes got to the dog, who after indicating she needed to go out immediately, had an accident. I was concerned about her health and about finding an expeditious way to get airport maintenance to the scene. But the reactions of others engraved the scene in my mind forever. I now know I can live through deep and prolonged embarrassment. First a lady stopped and opined, "I think it's awful she lets her dog do that." Then my mother, who had not grown up with dogs, ordered my father to wipe the dog's behind, and my father declined to do this. Finally the airline responded by seating me in a whole world by myself with blankets spread on all seats and on the floor. I wonder if the other passengers wondered what was wrong with me, or why I deserved this kind of splendid isolation.

Early in my traveling days, I learned the truth of the old southern expression "honey attracts more flies than vinegar." On the way to Pineville, Louisiana to visit friends from my internship at Central Louisiana State Hospital, I was transferring from a major airline to a small commuter airline for the leg into the Alexandria/Pineville airport. The commuter lines said that their planes did not carry "live animals." I was in my mid-twenties and a bit brasher than now. I told them that it was a federal regulation that they had to take this Seeing Eye dog. They repeated the "no live animals" rule; I repeated the federal law. They ended the conversation, they thought, by saying, "This is Louisiana. We don't have to follow federal laws." Clearly I wasn't winning this one, so I went back to the big airline and asked them for help. One of their representatives went to the commuter airline and applied some of his charm. He must have pointed out that no Seeing Eye dog had hijacked a plane in years and suggested that they try carrying her on an experimental basis. After more smoothing of feathers, I enjoyed a fine flight into Alexandria. Laws are necessary, but that day I learned that diplomacy is just as vital.

My advice to travelers with disabilities is to plan ahead and keep asking as clearly as you can, but nicely, for what you need. For me planning ahead always includes a change of underwear in my purse in case my luggage gets lost and enough dog food for a couple of meals.

They don't sell dog food in airports, bus stations, or railroad stations. With the price of hamburgers in these establishments, I'd better carry dog food. Asking for what you need includes continuing to ask. Many large airports have special-services rooms where those of us needing special assistance are parked between flights. For those of you who have never spent time in such a place, I'll describe it for you. The special service room contains a TV set (usually on fairly loud and tuned to a game show), a wheelchair-accessible bathroom, and rows of uncomfortable chairs. The room also includes a desk with a harried airport employee keeping track of the paperwork on unaccompanied minors, internationals who need assistance because they lack English skills, and people with various disabilities. Sometimes someone slips through the cracks. I have seen a couple of grandmothers in wheelchair miss their flights because somebody told them to, "Sit here, dearie," and then lost track of them in the rush of other demands. I keep track of my own time and am "in their face"—nicely, I hope—so I am always in plenty of time to get assistance. I dislike the "special room treatment" but understand that this may be a time for me to accommodate the airlines' needs so that they can accommodate mine.

Travel after 9/11 has changed for all of us. My Seeing Eye dog's comb has been taken away from me by airport screeners because it could be a weapon. I've also been asked the gender of my dog so that the screeners could have someone of the same gender search her. "It's the rule," the official said unctuously.

For you would-be good Samaritans on the road, please offer help to those of us with disabilities. We can always say, "No thanks." Sometimes a simple, "I'm going to the snack machine—do you need anything?" can make a big difference. Think about the next time someone with a disability comes to visit you. What would they enjoy doing in your town? Dear friends in several cities have taken me to used bookstores, my passion since I have a reading machine, and spent an hour reading titles aloud to me in my favorite sections: animal stories and travel books. I also remember a waiter who just assigned himself to our table when about ten of us, including a quadriplegic woman, were dining out after a conference. He sat beside her, assisted her in eating, and even participated a bit in the wild post-conference chatter. Best of all, he acted like it was a daily event for him. Special tours, cruises, and camps exist for our traveling pleasure, but for the majority of us who travel beside you, it will be that little offer of help that will make traveling fun.

Since I was ten, I've adored seals and dolphins and dreamed of taking a trip to spend some time with real dolphins. I've read everything I could about these graceful, intelligent, and playful mammals. I've fantasized about someday having a pool of my own with a seal or dolphin in it so I could swim and commune with the creature in its own world. About twenty years ago, a friend of mine went to Key Largo to swim with the dolphins. I was a deep shade of green. In 2001, I finally took to heart the advice I give to others when I'm counseling them about making their dreams come true. I called Dolphins Plus™, the oldest swim-with-the-dolphins program on the Keys of Florida, and made a reservation. My Seeing Eye dog, Carter, and I flew to Orlando where we joined up with three friends for the six-hour drive to Key Largo. Two of us swam, one took pictures, and one walked Carter.

Dolphins Plus offers structured and unstructured two-hour swims, as well as three- and five-day mammalogy courses and internships. I opted for the structured swim. The swim aims to educate people about dolphins and give opportunities to have physical contact with them in their world. There are twelve dolphins at Dolphins Plus trained to work with people. My partner, named Kimbit, was a seven-year-old, 600-pound, nine-foot-long honey of a guy with eighty-eight teeth (none of which I felt, thank goodness). Before swimming with the dolphins, you hear a forty-five minute orientation lecture, stressing the intelligence of these sea mammals. It turns out that dolphins know which women are pregnant, and circle around them just as they'd surround a pregnant dolphin. One day, a lady swimmer was surrounded but denied she was pregnant. After she went home, she had a pregnancy test and, sure enough, the dolphins had been the first to know. They also know if someone has a pin in their hip. Dolphins have their own sense of how to treat people with various disabilities. Compared with his more rough and tumble approach with the sighted man with whom I swam, Kimbit was very gentle and slowed his pace when dealing with me. We were also told how to approach the dolphins: ease into the water and let them come to you.

The adventure began after the orientation lecture. Carter trotted off with a friend for an hour to walk, smelling anything he wanted. He'd seen the dolphins and a sea lion and was very impressed with what big "water dogs" they were. However, he was glad to go have a sniffing walk. I eased into the eighty-degree seawater of the pen, and the trainer called the dolphins over. Each time the dolphins did what they were asked, she blew the whistle, and they came to get their fish rewards. One time the dolphin was slow to grab its fish, and a lurking seagull snatched the fish out of the air. The dolphin clicked, whistled, and generally complained about the unfairness of life. The dolphins pushed me across the pool backwards and took me for a ride holding onto their dorsal fins. I got to shake their fins and dance with them. When the swim was over, Kimbit and I even exchanged a hand kiss. In case you've ever wondered, dolphin skin feels like a peeled hard-boiled egg: firm and smooth.

I recommend this experience to anyone who likes to get up close and personal with other creatures. Dolphins Plus is connected with Island Dolphin Care, a nonprofit organization which provides dolphin-assisted therapy to help children and families deal with various developmental, emotional, and physical disabilities. The fact that the staff was used to working with people of all ability levels and ages made it an affirming and positive experience for me. I didn't have to explain what I needed because of my blindness. I came back to Eau Claire to a week of counseling college student stressed out by midterms, but made it through the week with a smile on my face. I'd made a new friend, and Kimbit's grace, intelligence, and friendliness are still with me.

Another year, I attended a week of extension classes at the Rhinelander School of the Arts. The extra arrangements I made included hiring a university student to drive me up to Rhinelander and to spend five minutes showing me the closest plot of grass for the dog's relief. I also contacted the administration of the School of the Arts to have a volunteer walk around and show me where my classes were the first day. Because it's a state university program, the school has to be accessible, and they certainly were. I took food in my knapsack, not liking to eat alone in restaurants, but I really didn't need to do that. People were extremely friendly and I never had to eat alone. I took one taxi ride from the motel to school, but after that had more offers of rides than I needed from folks in the motel. For a single blind woman, it's a doable and not-too-pricey vacation. If you don't want to come clear to Wisconsin, check out your state's university extension system; it may have something similar. I took classes on writing comedy, writing children's books, story-telling, and stand-up comedy.

A new trend in the hospitality industry is blind restaurants. It fascinates me that you sighted folks want the opportunity to dine in the dark. I get a kick out of imagining you struggling to cut up spaghetti or canned whole peaches, and paying high prices to do so. Welcome to my world! Does the food really taste better?

For those of you who work in the hospitality industry, please ask those of us with disabilities, "How can I help?" Your training manuals do not cover all situations. Who remembers what's in them anyway? I may ask you to put a piece of tape on a key card so I know which end to use, or to show me where the police dogs potty in the airport. You don't have to know how to meet every possible disabled customer's needs. A general offer starts the ball rolling, and I'll take it from there.

Blindness Monologue: Going to the Bathroom

If you're offended by the mention of bathrooms and the needs of everyone to use them, please skip this monologue. Your time will be better spent reading something inspirational, like John Milton's sonnet on his blindness, or doing something to help blind people, like signing the back of your driver's license to donate your corneas.

Now that we are rid of the holy one percent of us, let's get real. There are only two parts of bathroom duty that prove unusually difficult for blind people: finding bathrooms and using them.

In the finding-bathrooms department, have you noticed that since the Americans with Disabilities Act was passed, bathrooms, like other important features in buildings, are marked in Braille? This does not help! Can you imagine feeling your way around a whole floor of a building looking for that one sign that says "women"? The people mandating these signs had their hearts in the right place, but they assumed that blind people could just glance down the hall like sighted people can.

In an airplane, there's the dilemma of which bathroom to use. If I'm seated in the front of the coach section by the bulkhead, where my guide dog has more room to lie down, the coach bathroom is clear in the back of the plane, but the first class bathroom is closer. Maybe because I'm a child of the 1960s, I go forward. Close is good.

After finding the bathroom, there are different sets of dilemmas depending on whether the bathroom is big or small. In a big bathroom, where are the toilets? For women (I can't comment too authoritatively on men's bathrooms; I've only walked into a few of them by mistake), there may be a room with sofas, changing tables, etc., with another room with sinks and towel dispensers before you get to the room with the toilets. If the bathroom is occupied, I can always wait to hear the flush and direct my dog that way. Or I can ask a general question like: "Are you the end of the waiting line?" Getting out can be a problem, too, especially if a blind person doesn't have a guide dog or hasn't trained it with the word "out." Remember the song, "He Never Returned," about getting lost on the Boston subway? "She Never Returned," about getting lost in a large bathroom, just isn't as romantic.

In small bathrooms, as on planes or buses, there's another problem: what to do with the guide dog. It's one of the few times I've contemplated the advantages of a teacup poodle. I remember one bus ride down a winding road. I staggered my way to the back of the bus, asked the seedy-smelling character at the back if he'd hold the dog's leash, did my business, staggered back to the front, and sat down to applause from the bus riders. The bright spot about the bathroom situation is that blind people don't have to see how nasty bathrooms can look sometimes. Unfortunately, the smell is an equal-opportunity offender.

Gentle reader, you can help! If you see a blind person walking around a building with a look of desperation on her face, just use three simple words, "May I help?" If she has a guide dog and asks you, "Where's the grass?" she may be wondering where the police dogs pee rather than initiating a drug deal.

Amazing Grace and Beyond:
Churches and Disabilities

I've always been one to ask, "Why?" and this has often turned into "Why me, Lord?" Luckily, I have not been alone in my quest for an answer from the management. Job wanted to reason with God about his losses of health, wealth, and family. St. Paul prayed for the thorn in his flesh to be removed.

Sometimes Christians emphasize Jesus's miracles and imply that if you have enough faith your disability will be cured. I remember once being invited to breakfast after church. As I was preparing to leave, the hostess grabbed my hands and started praying that I would be healed of my blindness. The scrambled eggs were great, but from my perspective the theology was even more scrambled. I was deeply offended, even though I knew she meant well. I said nothing then, but seethed privately for weeks. Finally I realized that if I had added "but thy will be done" to her prayer, we could have agreed.

Or take the sermon on John 9, given almost every year. My Seeing Eye dog and I go to church and hear another totally uninspiring sermon about the story of the man born blind, which usually includes at least one of the following common points:

- I knew a blind person who was amazing (climbed Mount Everest, was cheerful all the time);
- it would it be awful to be blind;
- Jesus's healing of the blind man was miraculous;
- the Pharisees were blind not to recognize Jesus for who he was;

- pray that you never act blind (insensitive) to the world around you.

Once, as I fumed through the sermon, I decided I had to do something. In my younger days, I might have picketed. Being over fifty, I have written out some background and some better ideas for how this sermon could be preached (which were published in *America* magazine), so it can inspire both the blind and the sighted in the congregation.

The Old Testament contains five views of blindness worth noting. One image is that of blindness as a blemish, which disqualifies one from temple service (Lev. 21:18-21; 2 Sam. 5:9). Blind people are also portrayed as groping and incompetent (Isa. 59:10; Deut. 28:29). Other Old Testament references suggest that God punishes sinners by blinding them or their animals (Zeph. 1:17; Zech. 12:4). But compassion toward the blind is a duty for good believers (Lev. 19:14; Deut. 27:18). Isaiah also contains multiple references to a God of compassion who opens the eyes of the blind (Isa. 35:5; 42:7; 42:16; 42:18–9). Together, these disparate images combine to form the message that blindness is a blemish that limits a person, that blindness is sometimes caused by God, and that blind people are to be pitied by the sighted.

The New Testament clings to some old views, but introduces two new views of blindness. Jesus heals the blind (Matt. 9:27–8; 12:22, 15:30–1; 20:30 and 21:14, just to name the Matthean versions). Also Jesus disputes the Old Testament connection between blindness and sin (John 9:3). However, blind people are still viewed as objects of charity (Luke 14:14).

One of the attitudinal barriers that bothers me is displayed in our hymns. Images of blindness equaling darkness, sin, and stupidity abound. Take that wonderful hymn "Amazing Grace," with its last line "was blind but now I see." I know that this is metaphorical, but what about those of us who were blind and still are blind? Are we supposed to cheerfully sing this? Or, "Oh For a Thousand Tongues to Sing," one of whose verses proclaims "hear him ye deaf, His praise ye dumb, your loosened tongues employ, ye blind behold your Savior's face, and leap ye lame for joy." My heart demands more than knowing that some day in Heaven I'll see. In the case of "Amazing

Grace" I can substitute "was bound and now I'm free" for "was blind but now I see." But I am not sure what to do with that verse of "Oh For a Thousand Tongues." I just stand and think that the church and all of us in it are not yet healed from our narrowness and prejudices. I pray we will be.

Charity toward blind people has been a tradition within Christianity. As early as the 4th century AD, hospices and cloisters for the blind were established to carry out this charitable mission. Fast forward to 1824, when Louis Braille, first taught by a local priest (even though he was blind and poor), invented a raised code for letters which enabled the blind to be literate. Braille codes for most of the world's languages exist, as well as for music, math, scientific, and computer notations. Christian philanthropy for the blind established early schools for the blind in the US in the 1800s and church-related publishing efforts in Braille like the Xavier Society, which was founded in 1900.

Theologizing about why people suffer (called "theodicy" in the trade) has long tried to answer the question of why there is suffering and, by extension, disability. The fact that a book like *Tuesdays with Morrie* was on bestseller lists for over 100 weeks shows that this is a concern of many people. Theodicy explains suffering as: God's will, punishment, test of faith, opportunity for character development, manifestation of the power of God, redemptive suffering, and God's mysterious omnipotence. A given individual may express several of these perspectives on his/her blindness. Theologizing about one's blindness may also be influenced by the degree of one's acceptance of the condition.

Thinking about the causes of suffering in general, and one's own specific suffering, can either help or hinder a positive identity formation. For example, Erin (1991) found that immediately after the birth of a child who was blind, twenty percent of the parents surveyed viewed visual impairment as a punishment for sin, but that percentage dropped to four percent as time passed. Initially thirty-two percent of the parents thought they had been especially chosen by God to raise their special child and this rose to forty-five percent over time.

In the last thirty-five years, various theologies of disability have been put forth. Most theologies start from the position that we are all "fearfully and wonderfully made," as the psalmist said. A disability is but one part of who a person is, and we all have different gifts. Disabled people are called to use their gifts for the service of God. After all, Moses was called to lead the people of Israel and he stuttered. Jesus cured some people with disabilities, but more importantly he talked to and associated with them. The Jesus who suffered on the cross and lamented "My God, my God, why hast thou forsaken me?" was resurrected. The resurrected Jesus still had wounds. People with disabilities can take hope and comfort from a God who suffers with them, but for whom suffering is not the last word. God empowers the daily struggles of people with disabilities both with the concrete limitations, which are part of their disabilities, but also with the societal attitudes that limit their participation in this world. But people with disabilities are not only "suffering servants"; they are also leaders. For example, St. Paul's thorn in the flesh may have been a seizure disorder. Temporarily able-bodied people should be struggling beside people with disabilities, not pitying or stereotyping them. People without disabilities should also be seeking healing from their able-ism.

Most blind characters in the Old and New Testaments, with the exceptions of blind Bartimaeus and the man born blind, are not central actors in the stories in which they appear. They tend to be one-dimensional objects of pity or healing. Images of "darkness equaling sin equaling blindness" and "sight equaling light equaling insight" were widespread in Old and New Testament times. They still are. The line in the hymn "Amazing Grace," penned over 150 years ago, "was blind but now I see," is still used as a shorthand way to say "now I understand."

How can people who see in the twenty-first century avoid treating people who are blind the way the Pharisees treated the man born blind? Consider the following:

- Look around your places of work and worship, your circle of friends, and your favorite places to play. If you do not see one out of seven people with disabilities, ask yourself why. After you've acknowledged that maybe you don't know the disability status of all the people you see and that maybe people with disabilities "don't want to be there," hunt for other explanations. Are there physical and/or attitudinal barriers you can find?

- Imagine yourself with a particular disability like blindness going through your typical day. What would you need to do differently? This will give you good ideas of what services you can join people with disabilities to advocate for.
- Watch your language. I'm not asking for politically correct circumlocutions like "visually challenged." There is nothing wrong with the word "blind." Please do not use it to mean ignorant, however.

The biblical injunction still stands: "Invite the blind to your feasts." I would broaden this to suggest joining organizations to work for civil rights for and with people with disabilities. Also make friends with people who happen to have disabilities. After the initial discomfort of working out the concrete details of the disability accommodation, you will be repaid for the extra effort by gaining a new perspective on the world.

Being a boundary crosser can help liberate and heal you as well as those you are crossing the boundary to walk with in solidarity. What would Jesus do?

For those of us born blind, or who become visually impaired at any time in life, John 9 also poses some challenges:

- Where is God in your blindness?
- How do you step out in faith?
- How do you deal with discrimination because of your blindness? How do these incidents impact your faith?
- Where are you on the dependence-independence-interdependence continuum?
- Are there ways you wish your faith community treated you as a blind person differently? How are you attempting to achieve these?

Living out that process is where the faith community comes in. Most churches nowadays have national and/or local committees on ministry with persons with disabilities. These give guidelines for church accessibility, they provide religious education materials about disabilities and for students with disabilities, and they give ideas for Handicap Awareness Sundays. The old idea of ministering to people with disabilities as objects of charity is gradually giving way to ministering with them, but sometimes it seems much too slow in coming. For example, many churches will make sure that a wheelchair user can get into the building and attend Sunday services, but they may not even think to make the pulpit or choir loft wheelchair-accessible. Unfortunately, all too often the after-church coffee is held in an inaccessible basement.

A pioneer in the field of working with churches in ministering with people with disabilities is Joni Erickson-Tada. After becoming a wheelchair user as a young adult, Joni wrote several excellent books about dealing with her disability from an evangelical Christian framework. She founded Joni and Friends Ministry, which, among other ministries, provides helpful booklets about how to involve people with disabilities in your local congregation. The John Milton Society and the reference circular from the Library of Congress (shown in the references section at the end of this book) delineate the offerings of particular denominations.

I have enjoyed reading scripture or lectoring in the churches I have attended. I practice beforehand to make sure that my Seeing Eye dog and I can maneuver from the front pew to the lectern and back without a lot of obstacles. But on one memorable Sunday I hadn't done this because I was reading with a man whom I knew casually. I had assumed that he would make the crooked path straight if necessary. When we finished reading, I picked up my dog's harness and walked toward the steps leading down from the lectern. The dog hesitated, trying to pick her way carefully among the many poinsettia plants clustered there. My fellow reader, being a man of action, decided that we weren't moving fast enough so he got behind me and pushed me to speed up the exit. The dog looked over her shoulder trying to decide whether or not to bite this guy who was pushing me. She decided that going for the jugular up front in church was probably not the right thing to do. She put her full seventy pounds of Labrador energy into shoving one of the offending poinsettias off the step and out of the way. My fellow reader jumped down to salvage the plant and my faithful guide and I sat down as red as the poinsettia. I don't know whether this man ever recognized that offering me his hand rather than pushing us like a wheelbarrow would have saved us all some memorable moments.

Sometimes interactions are embarrassing, but more often they are very positive. Both those of us with a disability and those without grow. Once my first dog and I went up for communion in a church where you knelt at the altar rail and they used real bread. I knelt and had the dog sit beside me. Along came this nice man with a plate of bread right at nose level. As the minister got closer, the dog's neck got longer. Right on the altar steps, I lied. I muttered to the dog, "that's not bread," probably committing some kind of heresy. The dog sure knew that there was bread coming closer by the moment, no matter what I said. So when lying didn't work, I used brute force. I pushed the dog down, grabbed my communion, and rose with as much decorum as I could muster. I knew that God was probably laughing; after all, God created the dog too. But I didn't want her to take communion and offend some people. When I left that church several years later to move to another state, one of the older ladies of the congregation stopped me to tell me how much she would miss us. She explained that at first it had offended her that "they gave the dog communion," but that she had worked it out in her mind that the dog was one of God's special creatures and it was okay with her now. I didn't have the heart to tell her that her vision wasn't good and that the dog had never gotten communion. Her faith, love, and charity had grown and I was deeply touched by her witness. If you don't see many people with disabilities in your faith community, please ask questions and get involved. They may need transportation to worship or an invitation to sit with you at the next church supper.

As my journey in faith continues, I find myself more likely to pray, "How would you have me deal with my blindness?" in a particular situation rather than "Why me, Lord?"

Kids Still Say the Darnedest Things

For Excellence, ask an expert. For Wisdom, ask a sage.
For Honesty, ask a child.
Words To Live By
—J. Van Dyke

As parents and teachers know, the honesty, freshness, and curiosity of children are qualities that can't be beat. My Seeing Eye dogs and I have been privileged over the last thirty years to talk to thousands of children across the country, from daycare centers through high school classrooms. I also answer questions in casual encounters by the cauliflower in the grocery store, and in airports from coast to coast. In an unexpected place like an airport, the dog draws children like a magnet and soon parents follow.

Children of different ages respond differently to disabilities. At age one, children begin to notice and comment on differences. "Puppy, uh-oh," said one child to summarize the situation when she saw my Seeing Eye dog in a grocery store. My guess is her mother told her that her dog couldn't go into the store; so when she saw my dog, she wanted to point out that something was amiss. Countless toddlers have also contributed to my dogs' enjoyment of church by sharing their crackers, cereal, and candy by dropping them under the church pew. Labrador retrievers make good vacuum cleaners, even if they are also highly trained Seeing Eye dogs.

Before age three or four it's hard for children to grasp that they can see me but I can't see them. Once, after I had explained that my eyes were broken and I couldn't see, a boy asked, "Can't my daddy fix them?" Apparently the boy's dad was an expert at fixing the unfixable. At this age, wish equals reality for children. I've often been told that children have a Seeing Eye dog, as well as numerous cats, dogs, fish, birds, and other pets their parents have no idea they have.

Around age four or five, there is a phase where children know that I can't see and know that they can take advantage of it. Once I was babysitting my oldest nephew and things got quiet, never a good sign at that age. When I called out for him, "Bill," there was no answer. So I decided to make jokes and act silly, until sure enough he laughed and I pounced on him. As it turned out he was decorating my walls with his mother's lipstick. The true beginnings of an artistic interest that continues to this day!

When I talk in schools, I have the chance to show older children what my life is like. I usually talk about methods of reading first, because I believe reading is so important to all of us. I pass around a book in Braille, talk about books on tape and a computer that reads aloud, and using a human reader. Braille appeals to kids as a secret code. As a child I could read in bed and not get caught, whereas my brother with his little flashlight was always caught. But because there are very few pictures and no comic books in Braille, Braille reading may seem less appealing. And since my computer games are all spoken words, I don't get to zap any monsters.

After discussing reading, I talk about ways of having fun that the children and I might have in common, such as bowling or swimming. The theme of the talks is "different and alike." When I bowl, I use a rail to guide my left hand up to the foul line so I can aim straight at the pins. My average is about ninety, which is impressive to the younger elementary kids. For swimming, I swim near the edge of the pool so I can keep myself oriented. Even very young children learn that they have to keep out of my way because I can't see to avoid them. Braille playing cards are always a hit, especially when I point out that I could cheat by feeling them when I deal, but of course I don't (values of education strike again!). Checkers (round versus square instead of red versus black) are also a hit.

The kids are always interested in hearing about activities of daily life like dressing, cooking, shopping, and cleaning. When I ask children how many of their parents yell at them because they come home and drop books, backpacks, and coats in the middle of the floor, I always get a lot of "yeahs." I explain that my foster kids have to learn quickly that not only will I yell, but I may also fall over things left in the middle of the floor and say nasty words. So they *really* need to make sure they put their stuff in their rooms when they come home. Recently, I received a crack on the head because someone's friend did not know that shutting the door was important to my well-being as I cruise around the house without using a Seeing Eye dog. It reminded me that my young guests also get to educate their friends about how to co-exist with a blind person.

My method of shopping is trading help from somebody once a month in return for a parking space in my driveway near the university, which, like most universities, lacks adequate parking. This demonstrates to children my interdependence with sighted people. My Seeing Eye dogs could get me to the grocery store, but they couldn't tell a can of corn from a can of beans, and they certainly couldn't find the cheapest brand. My favorite shopping helpers over the years have always done the little extras, like pointing out new frozen foods that they think I might like. Because ads and coupons do not appear in Braille magazines, I may not know what's new and won't have a coupon for it either. Also, for clothes shopping, the matching of my clothes (buying six pairs of the same of knee socks instead of one pair to match each outfit) and the need for friends to tell me if something looks bad makes sense to kids.

I conclude my lecture talking about the best part of being blind: the training and working with my Seeing Eye dog. Afterwards, we get to my favorite part of the talk, the questions. Younger questioners go for the concrete details, like "Is Sugar a boy or a girl?"; "Can she have puppies?"; and "How do you eat?" I have to tell kids that no puppies are for sale because all Seeing Eye dogs are neutered before their training. Trust me, I leave the details of that operation for the wiser sex educators like parents and teachers to explain. As for eating, I challenge the children to try closing their eyes and eating some time. As a blind friend once said, "If you bend your elbow your mouth automatically opens." Only with long stringy things like spaghetti does eating become a problem...will all of it make it into my mouth or not? I don't think this is a problem just for blind people though. I may be a messier eater than many sighted people, but the job gets done.

Another question I hear a lot is, "How do you tell time?" It gives me the opportunity to show a Braille watch, and check the time to be sure I'm not being too long-winded or interfering with something vital like recess.

Older children ask more feeling-oriented questions like, "Do you wish that you could see?"; "Is blindness dark and scary?"; and "When you were a kid, did other kids pick on you because you were blind?" In answer to the first question, I point out that there are advantages and disadvantages to being blind. When I get lost, I would like to be able to peek at a street sign. Or when I get a juicy, handwritten letter from a friend (my reading machine can't read handwriting) and I have to wait for a reader, you bet I'd like to be able to see. But as I point out, if I could see my Seeing Eye dogs, I couldn't have them. Also, being blind has shown me how good and caring most people are. The only way I can tell a one-dollar bill from a five-dollar bill is by asking someone, and only once have I been cheated in my fifty-some years of life.

To the latter questions, I reply: blindness is not dark and scary. It's just gray like a cloudy day. Yes, sometimes children made fun of me. But as the saying goes, "If it does not kill you, it makes you stronger." I would not be the advocate for disability awareness that I am now if I hadn't learned early to stick up for myself.

The question that distresses me the most and which is increasing in frequency as the years go by, is "Has anyone tried to hurt you?" I explain that Seeing Eye dogs are not trained to attack, but each of my dogs has protected me when they had to. I wish we could live in a world where that didn't happen, and where second graders didn't have to think about things like that.

After the last question has been answered, I usually ask a "quiz" question like "If you wanted to write me a thank you note, how would you do it?" Of course, this is shameless begging for cute kid notes, but I can justify it pedagogically since I am helping them summarize what they've learned and reinforcing social skills like writing thank-you letters. After planting that seed, my Seeing Eye dog and I depart with many admiring glances, usually in her direction. She also takes a last sniff at the lockers as we pass to see if someone may have left a sandwich exposed.

Audiences full of teenagers are trickier. If we can get past the "I won't be impressed by anything a gray-headed woman could say" attitude, teens have many of the same questions and concerns as other human beings. I can remember how threatening it was to be seen as different at this age, so I really treasure the teenagers who will take a risk and ask a question, or make a comment about what their life would be like if they had a disability.

I often talk to students about becoming a Diversity Star; learning to embrace differences instead of just tolerating them. There are four steps to becoming a Diversity Star:

- Self-assessment and self-esteem: I am somebody, you are somebody, and together we can make a difference.
- Take small steps out of your comfort zone.
- Treat others with tolerance.
- Read, research, and reflect.

After I've done and said all I can, the feedback letters that I receive tell me a lot about the children, and how they put it all together. A composite letter follows:

Dear Dr. Schneider:

Thank you for talking to our class. It sounds scary but after a while I guess you get used to being blind so I would not be scared. If I see you walking, I'll stop and talk to you. I have three dogs and seven cats. In some ways it would be neat to be blind, playing cards. I've never seen a blind person before. I have a dog but it's not half as smart as your dog. Counseling fits you perfectly. My father had a collapsed lung. I think if you were in a reading contest, and they got to read words, and you got to read Braille, you would win. Now everyday I close my eyes and walk around my house but I always bump into my mom. What would happen if Sugar had babies? It would be hard to be a blind person because you would

have to know where everything is and your dog would
have to be alert so nothing happens to you.

Bye for now.
P.S. Write back soon!

Do You Ever Adjust? Self Image Questions

I grew up hating being blind. It made me look different. I lugged a Brailler and Braille books around school and used a cane. When I was little, I would to stare at pages of print through a magnifying glass hoping to be able to read the letters, or even just see that they were there. My parents didn't want me to "act blind." They discouraged blindisms, such as rocking or pushing on my eyes to cause visual sensations. These blindisms were punished with shaming, and it spread to being ashamed of being blind. I certainly wanted nothing to do with blind people…not that I knew any personally anyway.

As I became more independent, I began to take some pride in my coping skills. Various liberation movements of the sixties helped. I could be "far out" as the only protester with a cane at a peace rally, or by smoking pot for the visuals, which I experienced even though I couldn't see.

When I developed acute glaucoma in my twenties, I had to fight to keep my eyes. It made me realize that even if they couldn't see, and did not look good to others, they were mine and I liked them. I began to take some pride in dressing attractively, using makeup occasionally and looking nice, if not gorgeous. Part of my well-being was still based on being an overachiever. I discovered this when fibromyalgia diminished my energy so that I couldn't do as much on a regular basis. Gradually, my self-esteem has gone from being skin deep to having a profound pride in surviving, coping, and just plain being okay with who I am. A spiritual, "Please be patient with me—God is not through with me yet," sums it up.

Sexuality is a part of self-image that is often problematic for people with disabilities. In his book *Second Sight,* R. Hine talks about having great worries in this area after he became blind; to him, sight was a vital part of sex. When I heard him on a talk show, I had an irresistible urge—which I resisted—to call up and quote the old German proverb, "In the dark, all cats are black." Contentment with my own sexuality wasn't easily achieved. Growing up, there were not anatomically correct dolls, and the "dirty pictures behind the garage" method of learning about sex wasn't available to me. In the blind community, there are jokes about grade four Braille (feeling up the opposite sex), because most congenitally blind persons can only learn about sex by feel. I was a quick learner with the sexual part of my marriage. The way "Mr. Wonderful" smells, sounds, and feels can make him just as desirable as the way he looks.

People with disabilities struggle to define themselves rather than being defined by others' stereotypes. These stereotypes are so negative: having a disability means you're incompetent, asexual, or in an institution, and they make it difficult to feel good about your-self. Even treating people with disabilities as "wonderful" and putting them up on pedestals places them out of reach.

Actual blindness is not that bad. Sometimes it's a pain when I am not able to look up a phone number without paying for directory assistance, but the fear of blindness is much worse than the reality. Part of the fear is imagining how to cope and learn new techniques. Part of the fear is also imagining how others will see you. From want-ing desperately not to be seen as blind, I've grown to holding my head up and saying, "Yes, I'm blind."

Leading many self-esteem and assertiveness workshops has made me think about what rights I have as a human being who hap-pens to have disabilities. These are the rights that I would suggest:

- The right to have feelings about my disabilities and express them; for example, the right to have a bad day sometimes.

- The right to equal treatment; not better, not worse, just different in some ways.

- The right to ask for help; that is interdependence.

- The right to privacy; not to have to explain ourselves or be Exhibit A if we don't want to be.

- The right to self-determination; to decide my own goals, priorities, and style.

The right to ask for help has been a hard one for me to learn. Because I grew up with the stereotype that blind people were dependent and pitiable creatures, I went the opposite direction as far and as fast as I could. I was so independent that one of my friends made me a wall hanging with the word "Ask" in Braille letters made of buttons to try to push me to grow in this area.

I've learned that being totally independent doesn't leave much room for God or other people, and can be quite lonely. I've changed enough that I will now ask for what I need. However, I still monitor the other person's reaction to make sure I'm not asking too much. As a friend said recently, "I just won't think to offer, so you'll have to ask."

Adjusting to a disability or chronic illness is an ongoing process whether the disability is recent or long-standing. In my normal activities, I don't often think about being blind, or others not being blind. But then someone will approach me and say, "Have you got a pen to write down this phone number?" or "I stopped by last night but no lights were on, so I knew you weren't home." Suddenly, I'll remember that lights and pens populate the world of sighted people, as Braillers do mine.

Adjusting is obviously a cataclysmic process with a new, severe disability. Denial, anger, and sadness circulate freely as one begins to adjust. When you're an old hand with a disability, these emotions still occur, but less frequently. For me, when I'm away from home, I feel more blind. I find myself asking for more help, and I become a blind woman with a dog, instead of Kathie with Garlyn. With a disability or illness whose effects change from time to time, the adjusting process is always new. This can be extremely frustrating. A person may be trying to plan ahead but doesn't know how they'll feel or function later in the day, let alone a month from now. For example, being an optimist, I usually plan for my fibromyalgia to be quiescent. Being a somewhat reluctant realist, I also schedule some down time before I teach a night class so I can take a nap if I need to. There is no easy way to adjust to a disability or an illness. However, there are attitudes that I can adopt, at least on good days, which make life easier. These include

- focusing on what I can do, not want I can't and doing it my way;
- looking for a laugh in the situation if at all possible;
- being thankful for what I've got;
- being joyful in the moment;
- being assertive;
- remembering I don't have to do it alone;
- remembering I'm still growing; and
- remembering that I'm more than any disability. I'm a human being made in the image of God.

These attitudes are easy to talk about and hard to live.

I was doing a program for our clerical staff's development day, which the Personnel Department had named "Being Content With What You Have." The program was oversubscribed. In a time of budget cutting and downsizing, in addition to all the usual family and personal crises, shifting the focus from what's wrong to what's right was just what people needed. I've never sweated a program so hard before or since. I wanted to focus on how to live with these attitudes, not just talk about them. The participants in the workshop laughed a lot, particularly about how each of us gets worried about things that end up not happening, and miss the daily good stuff. I shared my pet worry that haunts me when I travel: will my guide dog be able to relieve herself when needed? The answer has been yes 99.9% of the time, but I still take this worry on every trip.

Adjusting is done one day at a time with the help of God and friends. Or as one of my friends says, "Yesterday's a memory, tomorrow's a dream, but today's a real b—— sometimes." It's up to me whether each day is blessing or bummer.

The Media, or Why I Finally Bought a VCR

I've always been a curious soul, even though I know what curiosity did to the cat. Being blind makes it more difficult to get some kinds of information, which leaves me trying even harder to get it.

I have a love/hate relationship with the media. I love to lose myself in a good story, but often I hate the images of people with disabilities in the media and the lack of access I have to some parts of the media empire.

Throughout my life, librarians have been superheroes to me. Not only did they send me Braille and recorded books, but they also know how to find information, and I thirsted for that. My first boyfriend at age nine was the librarian at the Michigan Library for the Blind, ninety miles from my home; I never met him so it was indeed a long-distance relationship. He sent me, on my mom's request, the limited supply of Braille books available for children in the early 1950s. When I came home from school and found large black boxes in the front hall, it was like Christmas to me. *Brighty of the Grand Canyon* and other Braille stories allowed me to lose myself in someone else's world.

There were so few books available and so few images of people with disabilities in the books that those that had such images stood out. Books about Helen Keller and Louis Braille gave the impression that all blind people were also deaf like Keller, or long-dead like both of them.

The world of reading for fun opened for me when I started getting the Library of Congress Braille Library books through the mail. Talking books on thirty-three rpm records soon followed. I spent many happy summer afternoons lying in my room reading classics like *Little Women*. Popular books like the Nancy Drew mysteries and comic books were not available in Braille or talking book format, and I was left wondering what the other kids were talking about in those realms.

When the *World Book Encyclopedia* was published in Braille for the first time in 1959, my school got one. I read most of it, thinking I'd know as much as librarians. I assumed they knew everything in every book they had. I joined a teen book discussion group at the library even though most of the books they discussed were too current to be in Braille or recorded. Just being around book readers was exciting.

My mother did much of my reading in elementary school. For example, when it came time to read the *Kotex Just-for-Girls Pamphlet on Menstruation*, she read it aloud and dutifully asked if I had any questions. Of course I didn't, even though I'd followed about ten percent of the descriptions of female changes and about zero percent of the text about male physiology. Since there were no anatomically correct dolls then either, I had to await intimate contact to learn about the wonders of the opposite sex.

Teachers of the blind talk about the gaps blind people may have in incidental information. A few examples may clarify the kinds of information we miss: what's the symbol on a street sign for a hospital? How many panes are in a Microsoft Window trademark? What color is a ruby? These don't seem like world-shaking bits of information. However, the ruby question used to be on an intelligence test.

Another area that is difficult for blind people to understand is a how sighted person sees the world: shadows, perspectives, etc. I didn't understand perspective drawing, or seeing anything for that matter, until I took geometry in the tenth grade. The teacher drew a picture of a road going off into the distance on my raised line drawing board. "Why did you draw the lines getting closer together as they went into the distance?" I asked.

Another area of incidental information where I'm way behind is in the product information provided by advertisements. Braille magazines do not have ads, so I don't find out about new products there. Many of the ads on the Internet, like those infernal pop-up ads, are not textual so my talking screen reader can't decipher them. Being mainly a public radio and public television listener, I don't hear many ads there either. When it comes to finding out about new-fangled inventions like hybrid cars or red, white, and blue patriotic pretzels I rely on sighted friends to clue me in.

Visual beauty is another area where I'm clueless. Why is puce, which someone described to me as muddy pink, a color anyone would like? I stayed away from art and architecture classes for my humanities requirements in undergraduate school, but would like to know enough to stay alive in a Trivial Pursuit game when my team lands on art. A few museums, especially children's museums, allow touching of their art objects. One museum offered a class for blind students interested in art and architecture complete with raised line drawings of some of the master works. Visual art literacy may be possible for totally blind people, but enjoyment may be limited to sculptures and other tactual arts. A few years ago, Braille (meaning raised dots on fabric) was briefly "in" in the art world, but much of it wasn't real Braille. It was the equivalent of a three-year-old's scribbling instead of real writing.

When it comes to visual beauty, like matching colors, or knowing what style of lamp to add to the living room, or knowing how beautiful my Seeing Eye dog is, I rely on sighted people's opinions. If you enjoy visual beauty, don't hesitate to share it with a blind friend. Even if they don't have visual memories from earlier days, they'll still appreciate knowing what you're seeing. When a blind friend comes to visit, find beauty you can both enjoy. Does your town have a rose garden, a symphony, a farmer's market, a bookstore, or a library with a good collection of books on tape? Beauty is even better when it's shared.

There are still times when a picture is worth more than a thousand words. I was hunting for information on cats on the Internet for a report my goddaughter was doing. Somehow I got into a pornographic site. The title of the picture, "Hot Kitty," let me know quickly this wasn't a site with the information I was seeking. It left me laughing about another advantage of being blind: not having to deal with those images.

As time went on, readers did most of my school reading. Some books were on tape and occasionally books, like my calculus book in college, were in Braille; being able to read math proofs again and again as one can in Braille was perfect. Tapes were fine for most humanities and social science courses. Readers were great because they were scheduled. I knew I would not wait until the night before an exam to do the reading because I would not have a reader then. Readers also had the advantage of being interesting human beings, some of whom became friends. Taped books, on the other hand, have the advantage of being small and portable, but the disadvantage of listening to them is that it's a passive activity. I've slept through enough taped books to be able to testify that sleep-learning does not work, at least for me.

Probably because of early deprivation, I've become a bookaholic. Keeping up with professional reading by tapes from Recordings for the Blind or readers at work is very important to me. So when I had the opportunity to help test a computerized reading machine in the late 1970s, I jumped at the chance. At that time the machine was as big as a desk, cost $40,000, and didn't work very well. But in the early 1990s, I bought an Arkenstone reading machine. It is about the size of a typewriter, costs $4000, and reads quite well. It sounds like Hal in *2001: A Space Odyssey* and pronounces "psychology" as "sickology," but being able to read just about any book I want to is truly wonderful.

Many of the first books I chose to read were children's books about dogs, like *Sounder* and *Where the Red Fern Grows*; I had been waiting to read them since childhood. The reading machine only deals well with typed material containing only text. Magazines and newspapers are not feasible because of the ads interspersed with the text. Much is gained by being able to read any book, but sometimes something is lost. One book I read was *Rivethead* about auto manufacturing plant workers. The workers in the book talked as you would expect. To hear the machine using its expressionless voice to say words that your mother or mine would have washed our mouths out for using was amusing in itself. The machines are still somewhat temperamental. Mine was manufactured in California and does not like cold weather. It needs to be warmed up for about a half hour before reading in the dead of winter. Even machines have their quirks. As the company's support person in California asked: "Do you have heat in Wisconsin?"

Along with the reading machine, I bought two IBM-clone 286 computers; one at work and one with a modem at home. This enabled me to get on the information highway, at least in the slow lane. Windows and websites were the next set of challenges. Resources like email, discussion groups, and library card catalogs opened new worlds. Technology is truly wonderful, except when it's down. I tend to take it personally, as did my Seeing Eye dog. When I was learning to use the talking computer, something went wrong and I said "you ****!" aloud to the computer. Sugar ran in from the other room to see what she had done wrong!

Because gaining knowledge means so much to me, I love to share. I search the Internet to help a friend correctly price a rare coin for a thrift sale. I encourage guests to touch the animal carvings I collect.

Another high-tech toy I enjoy greatly is Franklin Language Master's talking dictionary and game machine. Before I got it, I sat in judgment on the younger generation's being hooked on computer games. The first night I got it I was almost late for dinner at a friend's house because I was playing hangman on it. The cost, about ten times that of a nonspeaking model, caused me to wait about a year before buying it. But I think I've gotten my money's worth out of it. I've been able to use it to impress the hard-to-impress teenage audiences to whom I sometimes speak. The game machine and the Seeing Eye dog, a nice high-tech, low-tech combination, put me into the category of "awesome" with this hard-to-crack market.

Movies were another challenge to me. Of course I wanted to go because everybody did, but cartoons (which are highly visual) had little to offer me. Then along came *Patch of Blue,* about a white blind girl who fell in love with a teacher who was Black...pretty radical for the early 1960s junior high school student. Of course, the blind girl was played by someone sighted and did some things that blind people do not do. When going to movies with sighted family or friends, I was embarrassed about asking for clarifications of what was happening, so I kept my questions to a bare minimum. Movies were okay, but no great joy for me.

Accessibility began to increase in theaters, on television, and in videos with the advent of described theater and television. At the theater (in a few places), blind theatergoers can wear headsets and hear costumes, sets, and actions described. With a special television receiver, in certain areas, about five hours per week of public television programs like "Mystery" are described. To know who got shot really makes a difference in the enjoyment of a mystery. There are now several hundred VHS-format videos as well as some DVDs that have descriptions added in the quiet parts. The first time I watched one of these, "Dead Poets' Society," the description was so wonderful I finally understood why people enjoy going to the movies. Just a few videos are done at this point, but the technology is in place.

The images of blind people, or any disability group, are still light years behind the times. For example, two recent movies, *Blink* and *Scent of a Woman*, have sighted actors playing blind people. Even if an actor or actress has had six weeks of training to play a blind person, they do not do it as well as a blind person who's been at it for years. We are struggling to go beyond having white people play Blacks, Hispanics, and Native Americans, but somehow even though blind actresses and actors are trying to make a living, we have sighted people playing blind parts. That makes me want to picket.

A documentary on public television's *Point of View* shows how behind the times the images are. It was advertised as being about a blind woman who rides horses and is no "goody-goody." Ninety minutes of documentary focused mainly on her sex life and had several scenes of her in her underwear to prove she was a sensual/sexual human being. I think it's sad that this was newsworthy enough to merit a documentary. Have telethons (or pitythons, as some disabled people call them) really influenced the public so much that the "cute kid" image has to be fought with the "sexy woman" image?

When a friend offered to give me an old color television, I accepted and decided to get a VCR. Black and white sets were enough before, but lobbying from my father helped me decide to go with the color set. When VCR shopping, I tripped over another accessibility barrier: most VCRs have on-screen programming which is visible but not audible. Because of that I got a VCR player with no recording possible. The few times I've wanted something recorded, I've asked sighted friends to do it. Of course, some of them have trouble recording unless their kids are around to help them set the VCR.

If I were queen of technological accessibility, I would mandate that all television programs have both closed captions for the deaf and descriptive video for the blind; ditto for videos. If it were routinely done, it would not be that expensive. New computer programs and applications would also not be publishable until they were accessible to speech, with the exception of pictures. I would not require all video arcade games to be accessible, or all slot machines, but at least one in each group would have to be speech driven (for those who can't use Keystrokes) and have speech output for blind users. To solve the problem of "accessible to whom," the company could have a universally accessible workstation (open to wheelchair users as well as blind, deaf, and learning-disabled users). Such workstations are available now. Hasn't the time come to tell manufactures and employers that they can't say, "You can't play" to anyone?

Health Care Professionals: Without Whom This Book Would Not Have Been Written

When my mom fell down the stairs at a friend's house, five months pregnant with me, she was told to go to bed for the next four months to save the pregnancy. Thus began the impact of health care professionals on me. I was born a month premature and spent my first month in an incubator. In 1949 it wasn't known that the enriched oxygen atmosphere in an incubator would cause blindness. At least one lawsuit was filed against physicians and a hospital by a person blinded in this way. A large out-of-court settlement was received. The way I look at it, the health care community did the best they knew and without enough oxygen, I would have died.

Early in my life, my parents took me to several ophthalmologists to see what could be done for my vision. Family folklore has it that I could smell a hospital as we entered and would begin howling. These early traumatic experiences may have led to my current healthy lifestyle so I don't have to go to doctors much now. By about age five, it was clear that nothing could be done about my vision. For the next twenty years my forays into the health care system were for tonsillitis, sprains, and the usual childhood ills.

In my early twenties, I developed acute glaucoma in one eye—caused, I'm convinced, by birth control pills. In seeking treatment for this condition, I encountered the first truly insensitive physician I'd met, who said "Your eyes aren't doing you any good; let's take them out." I was horrified! They were my eyes. I was attached to them, psychologically as well as physically. It turned out that a simple operation relieved the pressure and allowed me to keep my eyes. True, they are not the best looking big brown eyes around, but they did come with the package.

As a partial repayment for all the good care I have received, I'd like to offer a few suggestions to those of you working in medical settings. *Business and Social Etiquette,* listed in the reference section, has wonderful coverage for medical people working with each disability, so I'll confine myself to a few suggestions that would really help.

- Greet me and introduce yourself when I enter your area. It makes me feel a lot more reassured to know that you are Nancy, a med tech who is going to draw blood, rather than just some wandering vampire. Saying "hi" when you're entering my room in a hospital or if I approach your reception desk alerts me to the fact that someone is there. You know you're there, but I don't...unless you had a lot of garlic for lunch!

- Read me instructions. If they're at all complicated, give me a Braille or tape-recorded copy to take home, because I may not have someone at home to read printed instructions to me. Please give me instructions I can follow. Imagine the frustration I experience from the following directives:

    "Take the pink pills twice a day and the blue ones four times a day."

    "Cut small pills in half."

    "Read the instructions above the toilet to prepare your urine sample."

- When I arrive, have office staff offer to help me fill out patient information and consent forms in a private place, so I'm not shouting personal information in a crowded waiting room.

Remember that when I'm on your turf I'm out of my familiar territory. Something that you do five times a day is strange and scary to me. At least every few years I believe each of us should spend a day being a consumer of the type of services we provide. Sensitivity training is often given to nurses and physicians in training, but I think all of us can forget how it feels to be a patient. In my own field when

I've sought counseling, I've been reminded of how much the little things mean. A friendly receptionist, help with insurance forms, asking if my panting Seeing Eye dog would like some water before we trot home on a hot August day: these gestures go beyond the "do no harm" of the Hippocratic Oath to make a healing interaction.

If you're the veterinarian or other animal health care provider who comes into contact with a guide dog, here are a few additional suggestions to consider:

- Be as flexible about appointment times as possible, so I can fit it into my work schedule and go when I can get transportation to your clinic. If my dog will be out of service for some time, work with me in scheduling this down time.

- During the first visit, gather information about my dog's work life, such as how much we walk each day and where we spend most of our working hours. When examining my dog, tell me what you are doing, and keep me with the dog if at all possible. This calms both the dog and me.

- If the dog needs special treatment or medication, explain work implications of the treatment or medications to me. For example, will this make my guide dog lethargic?

- Explain and demonstrate medication and treatment procedures to me. If possible, let me administer the first treatment while you watch and provide feedback.

- If small pills need to be cut up, offer to do this for me. Give verbal descriptions of signs and symptoms of problems to me in ways that I can use. For example, "stool is consistency of mashed potatoes" rather than, "stool is black and tarry."

- Ask about my dog's work performance. Look for changes over the years. Also, remember that vaccination recommendations may differ from state to state. For example, my guide dog was trained in New Jersey and we now live in Wisconsin, so make your recommendations accordingly.

- Be straightforward with me about indications you see that my dog might need to be retired. If you or others have concerns about my dog's work, discuss them openly with me.

- Consider giving a working dog discount. This is particularly helpful to students and those on fixed incomes.
- Be an advocate for guide dogs in your locale by educating your community on the Americans with Disabilities Act and guide dog etiquette.

Compare and Contrast

If you had to choose, would you rather be blind, deaf, or quadriplegic? Which is worse: to have seen and lost your sight, or to never have been able to see? Since humans have such large brains, we sometimes like to grapple with imponderables like these. When I'm asked such questions, I usually end up saying, "I don't know which is worse, but I'd choose the disability I have now." The devil you know is better than the devil you don't know. Then I think: at least I can still hear the crows caw or take a walk when I get frustrated.

Life with blindness seemed quite straightforward until my early forties, when I developed extreme fatigue and pain all over. I was worried. I knew a blind woman who had developed multiple sclerosis and I admired her, but I did not want to walk in her brave footsteps. Then a college student came to see me with the same symptoms and said that she had recently been diagnosed with fibromyalgia. I am often very empathic with people's concerns, but this time she complimented me by saying, "You're great! You seem to know just how I feel." I sagely counseled her about portioning out her energy carefully, prioritizing, using short cuts, and taking elevators when possible. Being an adult student used to overachieving, she did not like what I was saying, but said she'd try to follow my advice because she could no longer do it all.

What finally broke through my own denial was the day coiling up a hose and dragging it to the basement for the winter took me an hour. It left me totally exhausted and I figured that even being middle aged couldn't account for feeling that awful.

After a thorough physical and plenty of blood work to rule

out Lyme disease and multiple sclerosis, I was diagnosed with fibromyalgia and placed on low doses of antidepressants to help me sleep through the night. The medication worked and I began to feel like myself again. My battle to accept that I had another disability in addition to blindness began.

The first issue I had to deal with was fairness. Wasn't one disability my fair share? Why two? I had comebacks ready for comments like, "This will make you a better person." *If that was true, I'd be better already!* "God will walk beside you in this." *What about when I'm too tired to walk?* "You will learn from this." *Can't I learn some other way?*

The second issue was a practical one. One of the ways I'd always coped with the limits of blindness was to overachieve. For example, if most people read twenty books a year, I'd read twenty books a week. I was worried I would no longer have the energy to do this. I thought I had overcome the need to overachieve in order to prove myself, but fibromyalgia was going to test that assumption.

I also began to personally discover the disadvantages of an invisible disability. If people can't see it, they often assume that you're crazy, lazy, or whining for sympathy. After hearing, "Well, I get tired too," and "That's not really a disability, is it?" I began to be very selective about the people I told.

I also began to deal with fibromyalgia the academic way: by becoming an expert on it. I joined the Fibromyalgia Association, participated in the Internet discussion group about it, went to a local support group, and organized an on-campus support group in addition to reading everything I could about it. I learned that fibromyalgia is a chronic condition caused by lack of stage IV sleep, manifesting itself in symptoms like pain and fatigue. Fibromyalgia often runs in families and can sometimes be triggered by injury, illness, or extremely stressful situations. Treatments include medication, exercise, and stress management. Most people feel much better if they can re-establish deep sleep. Remissions and relapses occur for unknown reasons.

Armed with these bits of information, I began working out my own treatment plan. During summer vacations when I can nap and exercise at will, I rarely take medication. During the school year, I end up taking medicine about half the time and somewhat limiting my schedule. I fade fast after dinner, so I try to avoid giving presentations in the dorms late at night. Most students may be awake then, but at that hour, I'm about as exciting as a piece of furniture. There are still times when I do not do well at conserving my energy and I'm too tired even to brush my teeth before going to bed, let alone floss.

So what can well-intentioned friends of someone with an invisible disability do? First of all, believe them. They know what they are experiencing and what they should and should not be doing. Second, honest offers of help are welcome, even if not always accepted. A friend once asked, "How about if I come over and help you clean the fridge?" We had a nice visit and I got something done that I did not have the energy to do. Then we had a few good laughs about the green refrigerator objects we found.

What can those of us with invisible disabilities do? We can be honest about our limitations even if saying "no" is very hard sometimes. We'd better get used to the fact that explaining our limits to others and asking for help again and again will become a way of life. Although others can't read our minds, they will usually be accepting and helpful if we help them understand.

We need to accept our own feelings. Living with a disability is hard, especially when the disability is not visible. It will make you angry, sad, and frightened at times. The uncertainty factor with a disability that can change hourly adds frustration, too. Walk, swim, journal, join support groups, cry, scream! Do what it takes to get your feelings out so that you don't end up stewing over them. Prunes should be stewed; emotions shouldn't. Learn all about your disability. Become an expert on listening to your body as well as listening to what the experts say. Even if you've been recently diagnosed, you probably have more personal experience with the illness or disability than your doctor has. While they may know what typically works, you know what is right for you.

Find the pearls in this experience of disability if and when you can. While dealing with fibromyalgia, I've found more empathy with others' suffering and gained second-hand courage watching people struggle with it and achieve great things. One member of our campus group graduated with honors. I've also developed a little more patience with myself. I'm still diving for more pearls from it, sometimes by lying flat on my back!

Thoughts on Health, Illness, and Wellness

First, let's define our terms:

Health: a sound physical or mental condition; well-being

Illness: a sickness; a specific disease

Handicap: a disadvantage that makes achievement difficult

Disability: an inability to perform because of illness, injury, or malfunction

Syndrome: a group of signs and symptoms that occur together and characterize a particular abnormality

Wellness: satisfactory condition; recovered from disease

"Have you been well lately?" is a simple question. However, for those of us with chronic illnesses and disabilities, it is sometimes a hard one to answer. Most of us say, "Yes, and you?" and leave it at that. But when we're waxing philosophic or needing something to think about while using the rowing machine, it may be worth a few minutes of thought to consider "what is well for you?"

When I used to teach Wellness at a university—the first and probably only time in my life that this couch potato taught a physical education course—we discussed five areas of wellness: physical, mental, emotional, social, and spiritual. I like this broad-based definition, because even if you're not so hot in one or two areas, you can still be well in some areas. Often mental attitude and spiritual well-being are two areas where I do have some control.

A vicious cycle can develop when I don't feel physically up

to par. I get down about it and I isolate myself. Time for an attitude adjustment! Usually, the key question for me is: "Am I doing all that I can do?"; not "Am I doing what others are doing?" Things that help me get this perspective back are: walks, preferably with sunshine and birds singing; prayer time; listening to and singing along with old hymns like "Farther Along We'll Know All About It" and "Some Glad Morning"; petting the dog; and taking a good hot shower. Sometimes it takes throwing a pity party for myself first. The pity party preferably involves eating chocolate.

Another part of wellness is treating yourself well. I've had massages, taken a pottery class, studied yoga, and learned to crochet (sort of) to just plain pamper myself. It works! As long as I keep my mind on the goal of having fun, not on the outcome (like whether the crocheting is good enough to sell), it's fine.

I think the Special Olympics, with each person getting a medal, highlight a key aspect of wellness: being proud of just having tried. I'm not suggesting we all need medals for getting up in the morning or for not biting someone's head off when we're in pain, but occasionally we do. I'd like to suggest a few new events for the Olympics:

Olympic reception-going: holding a guide dog with one hand, juggling a cup of coffee and a plate of food with the other, and trying to make nice conversation

Olympic memory: having someone come up behind you, put their hands over your eyes and carol loudly, "Do you know who this is? I met you ten years ago."

Olympic perfect answer: Having lunch with some friends and having a stranger walk by and say, "Your dog looks dead." What do you say? (Extra points if you can think of a clever response within ten seconds).

Wellness to me does not mean perfection. I may choose to do heart-healthy things like exercising three times a week and eating fat-free cheese. However, sometimes I may eat a pizza and have a beer instead of a tofu stir-fry. Is wellness important to me? Yes, but so are some joys in life, like chocolate.

I didn't cause my disabilities and I can only do so much about them. Some New Agers believe that we could cure ourselves of all disease if we wanted to. I disagree! I can cope, but not cure. Sometimes I just have to let go and let God take over. "Do your best and God does the rest," is a good motto. Remember, doing your best means all things considered. Work, family, and other commitments count too. Few of us can devote ourselves full time to our physical wellness.

Be well!

Never Alone: Seeing Eye™ Dogs I Have Known

After over thirty years of working with Seeing Eye dogs, my self-image includes four legs and a tail. Most people who have not met one of these noble creatures personally have some of the following stereotypes: they're all German Shepherds; they wouldn't chase a cat if one danced the tango in front of them; and when not in use, they lie in the corner like a doorstop. The realities are so much more interesting! Those of us who have had the privilege of going to one of the fourteen guide dog schools in the United States or Canada have had the opportunity to work with another intelligent being to accomplish the goal of finding our way around in a complex world.

For a guide dog to work confidently and competently in many situations, it needs an enriched puppyhood, and three or more months of training at a guide dog school. The dog's first year is spent with a family or individual, like a 4-H family, who takes the dog to places ranging from the discount store to the Little League game to church and to concerts so the dog gets used to all sorts of people in all sorts of places. Also, in the first year, the dog learns basic obedience. After this year of home life, it's time for the tearful goodbyes and for the dog to go on to training. Depending on the school, the puppy-raisers may or may not meet the blind person who gets trained with the dog.

When I decided to get my first dog, I was finishing my PhD at Purdue, and realized that my internship and future jobs might be in big cities. A dog would make me feel more secure, even though I'd used a cane successfully for twelve years. However, on the first day of training, when we went down a quiet street in Morristown and my dog, Cindy, slammed me into a tree, I began to wonder. After doing this, she turned around to look at the trainer following behind us to see if she had gotten rid of me and could go back to him. She'd worked for and adored him for three months—who was this strange woman at the other end of the harness who clearly knew nothing about dogs? But things got better, and by the end of the twenty-six day training period at the Seeing Eye school, I left with my first Labrador, fully convinced that we could walk on water...at least in the winter!

Cindy was "the perfect one" I needed her to be. When I got her, I was newly divorced and just beginning my career as a psychologist. I had a doctorate in clinical psychology, a Seeing Eye dog, and very little confidence in myself or trust in others. She quietly and regally led me through my internship at a state mental hospital, five years of teaching and counseling at the University of Arkansas at Little Rock, and one year as a counselor at Iowa State. My trust in her rose, as did my self-confidence and love of others. Through her devotion, she taught me to love and to let myself be loved.

Some of the lessons she taught me are as clear today as the day they happened. One day, we were walking to work in the hot summer sun in Arkansas. The temperature and the humidity were both in the nineties. As we crossed a field, Cindy began to walk slower and slower. Being a Northerner by birth, I did not intend to slow my pace. "Cindy, hurry up!" I growled. "Come on! Let's go! Hurry up!" As the pitch of my voice rose, her pace slowed. We neared the middle of the field and Cindy stopped. Then, she did the unthinkable; she sat down. I fumed. As sweat rolled off me like a river, I berated her. What kind of a Seeing Eye dog was she to go on a sit-down strike? Still, she sat stolidly on the ground. Finally, it began to dawn on me that I was going to have to do something different. After all, I couldn't carry or lead her. I said, ever so sweetly, "Cindy, you must be hot." Her intelligent head cocked to one side in interest. I suggested kindly that she get up and we could ease on over to work where it was air-conditioned. She did. This incident started me thinking: if it worked to be nice and affirming to an animal, maybe it would work with people too. Not being a real quick learner sometimes, it was years before I learned to be affirming with myself.

So, Cindy and I walked through eight years of life together. She snored through many fine lectures of mine and walked regally past pastry carts in fine restaurants with my parents and me. When Cindy began to slow down, I went to the vet to see what was wrong. After a thorough exam, the vet said nothing was wrong with her but old age. I could either slow down or retire her. I was devastated. Of course, I knew dogs didn't live as long as people, but Cindy was my best friend, my eyes, and my transportation rolled into one gorgeous Yellow Lab body. As I worried and prayed about the decision, I began to stutter for the first time in my life. I could imagine Cindy resting serenely on a patio in the sun, but how was this going to happen? When some dear friends in Arkansas agreed to retire Cindy at their house, complete with patio and chicken added to her dog food, my prayers were answered. I called Seeing Eye with a catch in my voice and asked to be put on the waiting list for one of the popular summer classes. Then, I arranged my flights from Iowa to Arkansas (where I dropped her off), and then on the next day to Newark to start training with a new dog. As I flew to Newark without Cindy, I felt naked without that warm and loving presence at my left side. I knew she would be eased into the retirement lifestyle by a loving couple who would treat her like a queen. Later, they said that the first day she wandered around like a lost soul, but after that, she enjoyed the slower pace and less demanding job of being a house dog. When I went back to see her a year later, she knew me and was glad to see me, but made it clear that retirement was agreeing with her very well indeed. A few pounds, added to her frame from that good southern cooking, added to her dignity.

Meanwhile, I was at the Seeing Eye school getting matched and trained with Beth. I found out that no two dogs are alike, just as no two people are. Beth's love of life bounced out of her in waves. She started a fight under the dining table at the school when one doughnut crumb hit the floor where eight dogs were lying quietly. She always worked well, but her favorite job was country work. Once, she led me on a log across a stream, practically prancing. Beth also had a big heart for family. From time to time, young women— ranging from pregnant teenagers, to battered women, to a mentally retarded young woman who needed to learn independent living skills—have stayed at my house from a few days to six months. Beth welcomed each with a wagging tail and an offer to play ball or listen to their troubles with a nonjudging lick.

All too quickly, seven years of working with Beth passed. I didn't really notice her aging until I was interviewing for a job in Scranton, a big eastern city (or at least big compared with Ames, Iowa). We were ready to cross at a six-way intersection at rush hour, and Beth put her head behind my skirt. As clearly as if she'd spoken, she told me "I can't do this for you. Please retire me in Iowa with a nice family." When I returned from the job interview, I sadly put out the word to friends in town and through the Humane Association: one nine-year-old Yellow Lab with a big heart and a love for children looking for a good retirement home.

Nothing happened. No word about a home for Beth and no word about the job. Patience is not my strongest point. After about ten days of waiting and worrying, I finally gave it to God in prayer. The next day, things began to happen. First came a call from the University of Scranton offering me the job to direct their counseling center. Then came a call from a family offering to adopt Beth. A couple of days later, another family called. After visiting both families, Beth made it clear she would like the family with two children, another Lab, and a Manx cat.

This time, the leave-taking was done Sunday after church. A friend drove me to Pennsylvania and helped me learn what I needed to know about Scranton in four days. Again, I returned to the Seeing Eye school for three weeks of training with my third dog, Sugar.

Sugar soon distinguished herself as a happy dog. Once, on a lovely spring day, she banged her head into a parking meter, and then looked around as if to say, "Who did that?" Over the seven years I worked with her, thousands of children patted her at the end of our disability awareness programs in schools. She made it seem almost fun to be blind. Her favorite working days were when it was below zero and there was a nice blizzard raging. Sugar really shone when getting me through the drifts on the way to work. She loved our five years in Wisconsin. The retirement party I gave her was judged to be one of the finest university retirement parties by the ninety folks who showed up. Our mail carrier, daycare kids, honorary aunts, and friends galore munched bone-shaped cookies and extolled the virtues of this noble Lab. Sugar retired to live with a couple on a lake where she could occasionally sneak off for a swim.

Immediately after retiring Sugar in May, I went for a fourth time to the Seeing Eye school and returned three weeks later with a bouncy young Labrador-Golden Retriever mix named Tatum. Six months later, Tatum and I started out for our usual Sunday morning walk up State Street hill. Sunday, November 17, was a cold, blustery fall day. I was working with her to slow down in preparation for the ice and snow season. She was pulling hard, but was under control. Then, suddenly, she jerked both the harness and leash out of my hand and ran into the street into the path of a car. I will never forget the thud I heard. The car that hit her did not stop, but another did, and helped me rush her to the vet. On the ride, I kept telling her she would be okay and kept feeling for some movement or breathing. There was none. The vet pronounced her dead on impact. I buried my face in her still-warm flank to say my goodbye to the sweet, smart, bright star of my life.

The physical, gut-wrenching, don't-care-about-eating, can't-sleep-much grief lasted about five days. Friends sat with me, ate with me, and walked to and from work with me if I would let them. Condolence cards, calls, and emails let me know I was still part of a loving community, but the aloneness I felt was palpable. The "why" questions haunted me: why such a short life for a wonderful creature? Acquaintances asked, "Aren't you mad at the driver who didn't stop?" but anger was far from my thoughts. I just felt an aching sadness, a huge hole in my life. It wasn't just the physical loss making it harder to get around, especially in the winter. I also missed my friend—a friend to share a patch of sunshine on the living room rug at noon, a friend to fight with over the electric blanket. The only bright spots were that I knew she had died instantly, and that she was in dog heaven with Cindy and Beth. A five-year-old at the campus daycare center where Tatum and I had read the previous week wrote in his condolence letter: "I put you and your dog under the rainbow in my picture."

My identity changed very quickly. I talked to a Cub Scout group the next week. Usually, they would have been crowding around, wondering if they could pet the dog. This time, the leaders had to ask them to move up to the front of the room so I could make my presentation about Braille and communicating with blind people. Snowbanks became something to block my way instead of something to delight in clambering over with a dog.

The Seeing Eye school staff, with whom I talked the day after the accident, were most sympathetic. Occasionally, this sort of thing happened. Yes, they would notify me of cancellations, but it sounded as if it would be February or so before I could get in to train with a new dog. Mid-semester would not be a good time to leave my job counseling and training students, but I knew I would go whenever I got a chance. I just hoped I would have the energy to work toward building a new team with the new dog when the time came. I knew the dog would do her part, but would I be ready to avoid crucifying her for making a little mistake? Could I avoid being an overanxious guide dog user, out of fear of hearing that thud again?

I got on the rowing machine in my basement to try to keep fit, and waited. People asked if I'd thought of pulling my old dog out of retirement, or whether I could get a dog off the Internet. "No" and "no," I answered.

One morning, I got the call I had hoped for: there was an opening in the January class. Yes! The next hour, at work, I counseled a suicidal student, and the following hour began making the arrangements to be at the Seeing Eye school for nineteen days. Christmas was coming!

January 4 came, and it was time to go, but a blizzard was coming, so all flights out of Eau Claire were cancelled. The vans to the Minneapolis airport for the rest of the day were also full. As I stood at the airport counter in Eau Claire, a man left after hearing the cancellation news, seemingly unperturbed. I ran over to him and asked how he was getting to Minneapolis. He told me he was driving and offered me a ride. I ducked into the airport bathroom with the friend who had taken me, and asked if the man looked like an axe murderer. She said no, he looked like a businessman. Sure enough, he was, but I would have begged a ride from Attila the Hun to get to the Seeing Eye school.

I walked into the Seeing Eye school later that day shaking. Sure, I had gone through training six months ago, but I had just been through the worst six weeks of my life. Was I ready? Before matching dog and owner, the trainers walk with you and talk about your preferences. I said I'd take whatever dog they thought best, but I did remind them of the fact that I'd had nothing but Lab females for over twenty years.

A day after arriving, the match took place. I walked down the hall to a lounge and came back to my dorm room with a dog that I hoped would become my best friend, eyes, and mode of transportation for many years. My bundle of joy was Carter, a Golden Retriever male with long fur. My heart sank. I put on a happy face and called friends and family with the good news. My dad, a strong Republican, was very concerned: was Carter a Democrat?

One training trip was amazing. We walked uphill and down right after an ice storm with another dog that was trying to distract us for a block. Carter just calmly loped along. My heart began to sing again. We crossed busy streets in Morristown, and Carter stopped on a dime, or backed me up when he needed to in order to keep us from getting hit. He was my friend!

The day I came home from training, a sighted friend walked to and from work with us to help me teach Carter the route. The next morning, there was a foot of new, unshoveled snow and we strode to work without missing a turn. The Christmas gift of confident travel again walked beside me on four golden paws. Each year, Carter and I celebrated a Christmas in January.

Part of the art of matching dogs and owners is to match potentials. To predict how an adolescent dog will mature, and what that blind person's needs will be in several years, is an art indeed. After I got Sugar, I moved to Scranton within a block of three crack houses. She had the opportunity to protect me several times. Carter and I lived in a nice Midwestern town where he had to learn not to chase the fat, slow-moving campus ducks. Part of the "magic," as any devoted pet owner knows, is working on the relationship. I talked to Carter, told him what day it was, what we were doing that day, and what he was doing right and wrong. I've taught each of my dogs to find stairs in unfamiliar buildings by saying "up" or "down." Then they get praised when they find the stairs. Each of them, at middle age (anywhere from five to seven years old) has figured out there's an easier way, and has begun showing me the elevator.

Carter distinguished himself early in his working days with his sweetness and eagerness to please. When I'd hear a crow, I'd tell him "There's our friend, the crow." Within six weeks, he was pointing out crows to me by stopping and staring at them. Another of his skills was smelling when something was done baking, and going to stand watch by the stove until I took the hint and took the perfectly baked cake out of the oven. He also always traded a toy for his meals.

When Carter and I entertained company, he went from person to person, granting them equal time to pet him. This also extended to doggie get-togethers with guide dog pups in training placed with families in Eau Claire. He considered it his job to be the genial host, spending equal time with each pup.

When he was three, Carter had several grand mal seizures and was prescribed Phenobarbital for the rest of his life. Luckily, this controlled his seizure disorder and he loped through seven years of working life. Each July, we celebrated another seizure-free year with a party. I sometimes joked that I hired the handicapped as much as my employer did, and that Carter was a special favorite of the Epilepsy Support Group.

As he aged, his carefulness changed imperceptibly to uncertainty, and I had to make the hard choice yet again to retire a best friend. A favorite playmate of his, a German Shepherd mix who also had seizure disorder, invited him to move in. She had a fenced backyard and two doting retired people as added inducements, and Carter readily accepted her offer.

Even though it was the sixth time I had been to Seeing Eye, I was impressed again with the staff's skill, dedication, and attention to detail and the new ideas in the training program. One of my favorite additions to the training program was the "leave it" command. "Leave it!" is said to a dog just as the dog starts to lose focus; it means get back to work and move on. Since training, I've applied this to myself when I'm in a situation I can't fix. When I say, "Leave it!" to myself, it means let it go and keep moving forward. My sixth Seeing Eye dog is Garlyn (French for "prize"), a cross between a Black Labrador and a Golden Retriever. Garlyn quickly showed me that she was a smart, sweet cuddler, and had initiative. After taking me from home to work the most efficient way, she began to show me other ways to do the route. However, if it was very cold, raining hard, or otherwise not enjoyable to freelance, she'd go back to going the most direct route. A fifteen year-old girl raised her, so Garlyn's hobbies include napping and shopping.

The summer of her second year of working, after three grand mal seizures in six weeks, Garlyn went on Phenobarbital, just as

Carter had at about the same age. The good news is that she became seizure-free. The bad news is that it really slowed her work, even after she adjusted to the medicine. After a consultation with the Seeing Eye school, we determined that this was unfortunately not a fixable situation. So at their recommendation I chose to retire Garlyn and go back to train with a new dog as soon as possible. As all of this was occurring, Carter was diagnosed with advanced lung cancer. Along with close friends, Carter's retirement mom and I took Garlyn and Carter to the St. Francis Day Blessing of the Animals. All of us needed strength for the journeys we're on: Garlyn into a very early medical retirement, Carter across the Rainbow Bridge, and the poor humans on that human journey of letting go and loving again. Carter crossed the Rainbow Bridge on October 4, 2005 peacefully at home surrounded by his Marge, Bill, and Kathie. Later as we were toasting him in root beer and talking, a storm ended and golden sunshine broke forth. He reminded us that he's up there looking down in love on us, as only a Golden Retriever can. I am blessed that Carter's retirement home will be Garlyn's, as well. I confidently predict that she will enjoy the big backyard, car rides, and the life of a pampered pet.

These six dogs who have so enriched my life are good examples of the positives and negatives of being blind. If I could see these gorgeous creatures, I couldn't have them. If the puppy raisers, trainers, and volunteers who contribute to the guide dog schools were not there, I would not be able to walk confidently into that next situation with a guide dog beside me. It costs about $30,000 to put a dog-human team on the street, and no government money is involved. I am truly never alone, not just because I have six legs and a tail, but because of all the people who made it possible.

Grocery Store Runs and Other Activities of Daily Life

Let's talk about food first. Friends would say I always talk about food first! Eating is one of the equal-opportunity joys of life open to all of us. But shopping is a little different when you can't see and there aren't coupons or ads in Braille magazines to make you aware of new products.

The blind minimalists I know who don't like to ask for any help go to a familiar store because they know what category of food is where. For example, they know where the bread is, and one loaf is as good as another to them. Another approach is to ask a store employee to shop for you or with you. If the store values your business, you'll get good help this way. In some towns you can hire a shopper; in Eau Claire these shoppers are called the "Bag Ladies." They take a shopping list over the phone and deliver the goods for about $10. This is also an attractive option for sighted folks who hate to shop or don't have the time.

When I shop for clothes, I like a sighted opinion. I could rely on clerks' opinions, but they may not have the same taste in clothes I do. If it's a big purchase like a couch or framed picture, I use the committee approach. If two out of three like it, it must be good.

I recommend the barter system in getting daily chores done. I have a parking place near campus that I don't need. I "rent" it to a student in exchange for shopping assistance once a month. No money changes hands, but a lot of learning goes on in both directions. Shopping once a month this way has made me very organized.

One of the first students I shopped with was male. I'm ashamed to say that I'm enough of a sexist to have thought he wouldn't know how to clip coupons or pinch pennies. He did! I even learned a few tricks from him, like the fact that ten pounds of potatoes are sometimes cheaper than five pounds. I also shopped with a female math major who could compute price per ounce very well, but was less creative about informing me of new items I might like. My Seeing Eye dogs go grocery shopping with us, too, and add their own unique comments. One day there was a man in the grocery store dressed up as a kangaroo; he was promoting a product. My dog spotted and challenged him. When a seventy-five-pound Labrador started barking her head off at him, he hopped right on out of the store!

At the store or when we get home, I have the shopper read me the recipes for any new items and identify which can is which so I can put it away in the cupboard. Some people put Braille labels on their cans. I just file them in categories in alphabetical order (for example, beans in front of corn, etc.). When people come to my house and wish to be helpful, they do not touch items in the cupboard. If they do, my meals could get unexpectedly interesting.

For cooking, lots of adaptive equipment is available, from special measuring cups to labels for the oven or microwave. Since I learned to cook when I was a poor graduate student and have moved many times, I don't use adaptive equipment. When I move into a new home, I get a sighted friend to show me where 350°F is on the oven dial and then I guess about the rest. Cooking involves using a Braille watch to time and using my nose to tell when things are done. This works fine until I have a cold, at which point things may get a little overcooked. I have copied a lot of recipes into Braille, and now often get new ones from the Internet.

My goal in cooking is good taste; I don't think about the appearance of the dish. I once took cold beet soup made of yogurt, spices, and beets to a summer picnic. The bowl came back almost as full as it left home. I was puzzled because I knew it tasted good. But a friend told me that pink soup just didn't cut it with most sighted folks.

Cleanup is another area where I need a little help from my friends. I can vacuum, dust, and mop by feel, but it once took a friend to point out to me that I had nose prints on the refrigerator door. Not surprisingly, they were at nose level of my Seeing Eye dog, who likes to eat almost as much as I do.

Haircuts take some sighted input too. I can't point to the style I want in a magazine, so I just tell the beautician I want it short and low-maintenance. The rest is up to her and to feedback from friends. The "What do you think of my new hairstyle?" question requires a high level of honesty from friends; little white lies won't do. No "It's fine" while thinking "Glad it's not my haircut." True friends tell me "You have a spot on your blouse"; acquaintances do not.

Laundry is no sweat. I wash everything except new stuff together. This is what thrifty college students do anyway to save their money to spend on books or something instead of extra washing loads. Matching socks is a problem I share with color-blind people. The strategy I've adopted is to get all tan socks. Then they all match each other and match my dog's fur as well.

As I hear the neighbor boy start up his lawnmower, I'm reminded of something else I don't do myself: mow the lawn. I do shovel the snow, but cutting the lawn diagonally to keep up with the neighbors is more than I can manage. I don't even quite understand why it looks better done that way, but I take it on faith. You sighted people are just plain strange sometimes! When it's all added up, including occasional rides and shopping trips, I have about an hour a week of sighted assistance for homemaking chores.

The little extras of daily life are important to me, too. I have paintings by my mom hanging on the wall as well as feel-able art. I remember a young blind woman, who was a housemate of mine while she was earning a graduate degree in rehabilitation of the blind. One evening we were having some friends over for supper and I asked her to light the candle on the dining room table. She hemmed and hawed, and finally admitted that she had never lit a candle in her life, so I would have to show her how. I verbalized as I did it: close the matchbook; strike the match on the back going away from you; feel around with the match head until you feel the wick; go up a little and hold it there until you count to five or your finger gets too hot; bring your hand away; turn ninety degrees and blow it out. If it didn't light, start over. I lit the candle, and the dinner guests, some sighted and some blind, got to enjoy supper by candlelight. I can testify that spaghetti *does* taste better by candlelight.

Fostering, or What I Do with an Extra Bedroom

For the last thirty years I've lived in houses or apartments with two bedrooms, and I have the kind of conscience that says, "You have more than you need, so share." Putting my conscience together with my spare bedroom has led to a number of adventures in sharing space and life with a variety of women. These women have ranged from plain university students to international students from three continents. I have also fostered alcoholics trying to stay sober, an anorexic student, a battered prostitute, pregnant teenagers, a blind student, and a cognitively disabled young woman learning to live on her own. They've stayed anywhere from a couple of days to a couple of years and have left me knowing a little more about somebody else's corner of the world.

Women have been referred to me by social service agencies and by word of mouth. For an adult family home to be approved by social services for fostering, the house and the person doing the fostering are thoroughly checked out, including doing a criminal background check. Because of social service rules, I have several smoke detectors in my home and a huge fire extinguisher.

Many of the women who have stayed with me have described my home as a warm and quiet place to recharge and figure out where they're going. I tell each woman that although I am a psychologist, I will not counsel her because I'm off duty at home. I've heard much more about their situations than their counselors.

I've become adept at stating my basic requirements up front, such as no illegal drugs and no men upstairs after ten at night, so I can run to the bathroom without getting dressed. Social Services also have requirements and will set goals with each foster woman. I may be asked to teach them to grocery shop on a limited budget or encourage conversation and fun at mealtimes.

People have often assumed that because I can't see and most of my housemates can that "they must be a big help to you." Probably as a reaction to this I've been very careful not to ask any more of them than a sighted landlord would. I do ask minimal things such as that they keep their junk in their rooms instead of in the middle of the living room floor, a request most moms would make. "Don't leave doors open where I'll run into them" is a request that makes sense immediately to all no matter what their intelligence level.

The houseguest who wanted to help me the most was the cognitively disabled young woman. She had lived in a variety of group homes, and this experience had left her feeling handicapped. She told me one day as we were doing some cleaning together that she couldn't wash windows because she was handicapped. I just handed her the cloth and said, "Yes, you're handicapped; yes, I'm handicapped; and yes, we will wash the windows together." We did, and I didn't hear the "I'm handicapped" and "I can't" lines again. After she got over thinking she couldn't do anything, she really enjoyed doing things for others. Unfortunately, after that young woman moved into an apartment, people started doing more and more for her, and she became more "handicapped" again.

Because of my life experiences I think I have a different view of what's required for independent living than some professionals in the field. For example, when I asked for goals for the cognitively disabled young woman, I was given a ten-page list that included: sorting clothes before washing them, using a bus schedule, and understanding credit. In my opinion, she didn't need to sort clothes—I don't and neither do many people who can only afford one washer load per week. Teaching someone who does not read to use a bus schedule is nearly impossible. Understanding credit is a trick that millions of Americans have not quite mastered. All she needed to know about credit was not to mess with it. But living independently, to me, does require being able to deal with other people's comments, an area that I could help her with. Because this young woman had some speech impairments and was a bit awkward, she was made fun of sometimes. This made her mad; occasionally, she'd get angry enough to take a swing at a tormentor. Although this was understandable, it could also land her back in some kind of institution. We talked about other more Christian solutions like praying for her tormentors. I wasn't sure how far we were getting on the subject until one day she came back from a trip and told me that someone had teased her at the bus stop, but she had handled it. I asked her how, holding my breath. She said she'd told him, "You're handicapped, not me." I was impressed.

Another memorable moment around the issue of what's considered "normal" came up one day when an anorexic young woman was living with me. I got a call at work from her social worker saying that there was a problem that she needed to discuss with me: I had some black bananas in the refrigerator. The anorexic young woman had told the dietician that the presence of black bananas in the refrigerator was why she hadn't eaten much that week. I admitted to the possession of black bananas and told the social worker that I planned to make banana bread with them. Then I asked the social worker if she had ever had black bananas in her refrigerator and whether they had kept anybody in her family from eating. She said she had some and nobody had shown any loss of appetite in her family, but this young woman was anorexic and needed special care. To me what she needed was to hear what I told her that evening: in this family, if you have a problem with someone, you tell that person about the problem, and then you work it out. I also told her that if my food ever bugged her again or was moldy or bad, I'd really appreciate it if she told me. She hesitantly agreed, and the black banana issue went away. It did make me wonder how much professional time went into discussing those poor dead bananas.

By fostering, I've also become aware of some of my own prejudices. When a woman from Hong Kong ate hot dogs for breakfast or a Central American used practically no soap to wash dishes, I discovered some of my unquestioned assumptions. After the battered prostitute asked me if she could come to church with me, I asked my minister. He said, "Not unless she's willing to change her occupation." I was surprised. It seemed to me that it was our job as Christians to love someone in her situation first and then help her rethink what she was doing.

Another of the "hot buttons" I've become aware of by fostering is my low tolerance for complaining. A British student thought our television was garbage—too many commercials and too little content in the news programs. After she found out I paid $10 per month for limited cable service, she practically went into orbit complaining. I suggested that maybe she'd like the news on public radio better and role-modeled reading instead of watching television. I finally told her that I'd be glad to disconnect the cable if she wished. "No," she said, horrified. "I was just commenting." I would still come home for lunch almost every day to find her watching more of that horrible American television. It made me realize how action oriented I am. I wanted to shout, "Just turn it off if you don't like it."

From my experiences fostering, I've been able to learn about other worlds. I have been able to provide a safe place for some women and teach them a few skills. I've also learned a lot about myself, including where I need to grow, such as in the area of patience. Anyway, it gives me lots to pray about.

But I Didn't Sign Up for This: Parenting a Child with a Disability

When you decided to sign up for having a child, chances are great that you didn't special-order a child with a disability. In fact, one of the reasons often given for keeping abortion legal in the US is, "What if tests reveal the fetus has disabilities?" On the other hand, some parents do knowingly adopt a child with a disability.

Children always bring surprises into their parents' lives but children with disabilities bring more than their fair share of growth opportunities to their parents.

The first set of challenges is likely to involve lots of contact with the medical professions. What can be done about the disability or illness? Can I have a second opinion? What is the future going to be like for my child, and how long will they live? So many questions and such a scary time! My parents took me to several university hospitals to hear the latest thinking on what's now called retinopathy of prematurity. Now many parents will also jump on the Internet to research their child's condition.

Soon after the initial medical flurry comes the next issue: educating the child. The alphabet soup of IEPs (individualized education plans), Public Law 94-142, Americans with Disabilities Act (ADA)-mandated accommodations, etc., is added to the newly mastered medical jargon of medical conditions and medications and treatments. Local, national, and online support groups of people with and parents of children with the disability become new mentors in navigating school and life with disability mazes.

But as you deal with the medical, educational, and day-to-day crises of raising a child with a disability, don't forget your emotional responses and those of your spouse and other children. The grief you feel because your child is not perfect, "normal," or whatever you call it, is completely natural. All parents worry about their children's futures, but those raising a child with a disability worry more. Some parents grieve by going through stages like those faced by people grieving a death: denial, anger, bargaining, depression, and acceptance. If the grieving process is not allowed to proceed at its own pace the process may get stuck. If the medical condition is progressive, you may go through the grieving process many times. Different people grieve differently and it is common for the disability of a child to highlight differences between two parents. One parent may be trapped in denial and the other may take over parenting entirely. A child with a disability can put much stress on a marriage and the marriage may dissolve or at least flounder for a while. In my parents' case, because of my mother's experience teaching the deaf, she dedicated herself to raising me; my father retreated to his work.

What about the other kids? Not surprisingly, they may feel resentment toward the child with the disability for getting all the attention, having less expected of them, etc., and may feel ashamed of being seen with their disabled sib. Of course, having a sibling with a disability can also bring many positives to the child without a disability, including appreciation of human differences, empathy, compassion, and pride in being a helper. There may also be conflicted feelings like gratitude for not having the disability, but fear they could catch it, and guilt for being glad they don't have it. To make the positive outcomes happen, the parents need to give the siblings plenty of information about the disability so the child can answer their own questions and their friends' questions. "Is it catching?" "Can someone fix it?" "Why do they act that way?" are common questions.

The non-disabled child also needs to know from the parents that they are not the disabled child's keeper and that they do not have to be a superkid to make up for what the child with a disability cannot do. Time alone with each child and talking honestly about the child's concerns about unfairness, etc. can go a long way toward creating the kind of family where the disability is just one part of family life. It may take center stage sometimes; usually, it can be on the back burner, but not ignored. Nowadays there are support groups and books both for children with disabilities and for their siblings as well. So what's a parent to do? Three key pieces of advice:

- At first the disability has to become your new hobby. Learn all you can, join support groups, track down adults with it.

- Realize that your family will no longer be anonymous like "normal" families. The equipment you have to carry, the visibility of the disability, etc. make quick trips to the mall or last-minute getaways with your spouse with a babysitter holding down the fort things of the past. Your organizational and planning skills, as well as your public speaking and advocating skills, will grow by leaps and bounds.

- Take time for yourself and your spouse. Like any crisis, a child with a disability can cause you to pull together as a team or pull apart. Use respite care, babysitting offers from extended family, etc., to get couple time even if it's only for breakfast at the corner diner to celebrate the last week's survival and plan for the next week. When your child with a disability can go to summer camp, make sure they go even if everyone is scared. Both you and they need the time apart.

An Open Letter to Young People
with Illnesses and Disabilities

Welcome to one of the largest minority groups there is! Like you, fifty-four million Americans have illnesses or disabilities. Perhaps you were given this book by some well-meaning parent or teacher who thought it would inspire you. Maybe you were offended and wondered what some gray-headed blind woman could say to you. Let me assure you: I'm not trying to inspire you or say you should live your life in a certain way. I'd like to share my experiences with two disabilities. One is visible (blindness) and one invisible (fibromyalgia). I hope you can look at them and relate them to your own.

Let's discuss being "inspirational." Life is sometimes inspiring and sometimes boring, with or without disabilities. There are times when each of us is at our best and a truly inspiring human being; then there are the other days! If you find some of my experiences inspiring, great. Be assured that you will have your own, and they will shine even brighter for you.

I grew up ashamed of my differentness. I hope you have not had this experience, but I'll bet many of you have. I didn't want to use a cane or be labeled as blind; I wanted to be normal and able to see. The fashion and cosmetic industries, among others, spend billions of dollars to convince us that we have to look a certain way in order to fit in. Don't get me wrong: I think looking clean, neat, and attractive is important. However, I've grown to realize that there's more than one way to be "normal" or "beautiful." My talking dictionary says,

"Beauty is that quality that gives pleasure to the senses or exalts the mind." This suggests that it's all in your own perception. I didn't begin to figure this out until my mid-twenties, when a mentor told me I was attractive. Until then I'd heard that "looks are not important," which led me to believe that people were kindly trying to say "it's okay that you're ugly." That mentor also showed me how to use makeup when I wanted to use it, but gave me the larger gift of feeling beautiful anyway. I'd learned that it is not wrong to try to be beautiful, but why not try for your own beauty instead of beauty like someone else's?

Part of feeling attractive for each of us with a disability is pride in our disabled part. Naming and polishing up your electric scooter can be as much a matter of pride for you as brushing my guide dog is for me. Exercising, working in physical therapy, and dancing can also help give you pride in your body.

If you're feeling in need of a self-image makeover, some questions you might like to ask yourself are:

- What are two things I'm good at?
- What was something I did that was really hard?
- What do I wish I could do?
- What was the kindest thing I did today?
- Who are three people I can count on to help me?
- What can I do when I feel bad?
- What am I thankful for?
- When is it hard for me?
- What can I do when I'm teased?
- What are some of the things my parents like best about me?

An improved self-image can go a long way in helping you set and achieve your goals. With that in mind, what are you going to do with your life? I'm not going to glibly tell you can do anything you want to do. Even if I really want to be an airline pilot, no law on the books will get me, or any other blind person, a pilot's job. This is not to say that I can't work for an airline in public relations, employee training, or reservations. Some limitations can be accommodated for, some cannot. You need to seek honest feedback from parents, teachers, and counselors about what obstacles they see in your path as well as what gifts and talents they see in you.

I considered several careers before ending up as a psychologist. One of the best things I did in my career search was to interview people actually working in the field. You can learn a lot from courses and books about a future in a particular career, but sitting down with someone who does this work every day makes it much more real. I suggest you make an appointment and take in a list of ten questions. It's okay to ask about the salary, but not as your first question. If the person you are interviewing happens to be a person without your disability, don't hesitate to ask if they can refer you to someone with a disability similar to yours who you can interview. It might involve a long-distance phone call or two, but it can be very heartening to hear how that person dealt with some of the problems you will face. When you think you've found the right field, volunteer or try to get an internship.

In case you've not discovered it yet, life is not fair! The playing field of life is not a level one. Laws like Americans with Disabilities Act and Public Law 94-142 can help you obtain equal access to education and employment, but we're not there yet. Seventy percent of people with significant disabilities who are able to work are unemployed. Not only is this unfair to them, but also to the working world that is missing their contributions.

I get angry as I write about unemployment and discrimination. Just like everyone who has faced discrimination, I sometimes feel like giving up. But most days I fight to change people's hearts and minds in what little ways I can. I may confront a tactless remark, such as "What are you, blind or something?" when the word "blind" is used to mean "stupid." I may need to force access in a restaurant that doesn't acknowledge that assistance animals are allowed even when I show them the state law. Besides individual confrontations, I can recruit allies. For me this can be done by presenting a program to a local service club about life with disabilities, or working with a legislator to change a law so that blind people can have the secret ballot that sighted people take for granted. None of these are far-reaching, Nobel-Prize–winning kinds of activities, but they do make a difference. As you live your life, these opportunities will come to you even when you're not looking for them. Sometimes they'll turn out the way you want and sometimes they won't. As the old saying goes, "It doesn't matter if you win or lose, as long as you suit up for every game."

Some days you may not feel like planting the seed of understanding or explaining yourself. When those days come, I recommend a good "pity party" for yourself. That might mean complaining to a friend about the unfairness of it all, taking a long walk, or enjoying a long soak in the tub. It's okay to feel sorry for yourself sometimes. If you don't, who will? After you've wallowed in it a while, you will be able to pull yourself out. Even if you're a "We Shall Overcome" kind of person, which I hope you are, remember that the next word in that civil rights song is "someday." That doesn't necessarily mean today. You're in it for the long haul, right?

What about friends and family without disabilities? Can they really understand what you're going through? I believe it's like musical talent: some folks are born with more than others, but it still takes practice for everyone. My experience is that most people want to understand and be helpful, but they are not mind readers. No one can understand how you feel until you tell them. Asking for what you need in a situation to be able to function is the right thing to do. That does not guarantee you'll get it, but it increases the chances. For example, I've gone to many conventions in cities where I've never been before and tried to get around quickly in unfamiliar places by myself. It's doable, but no fun. At one convention I asked for and received fifteen minutes of a sighted person's time twice a day to help show me around and read the late-breaking convention announcements to me. The people I met in this way were delightful, and the convention was so much more pleasant. I left wondering why I hadn't done it years ago. Perhaps I didn't because of some leftover shame at being different and wanting to pretend I wasn't.

One of the joys of growing older for me has been my increasing self-acceptance: "I am who I am, and that's good enough." Some people will like, understand, and accept me; some won't. When I ask friends not to call on weekends between 12:30 and 2:30 because I'm napping, some will think I'm lazy. I know napping is one of the ways I cope with fibromyalgia, and that I'm not a lazy person. I may explain it to them once, but if they don't get it, so be it.

Reaching out to others to ask for help or understanding is only half the story. The other half is reaching out to give what you have to share. You are a person with needs, but also a person with gifts. We all are. By reaching out to share yourself with others you will be doing a lot to chase away the old stereotypes. Stereotypes rarely survive in daily contact at school, work, and in the community. When we're out there working, playing, loving, and praying together, we all lose a few stereotypes and gain a few friends.

What Do You People Want Anyway?
Being and Not Being a Minority Group

There have been three ways of looking at any disability, including blindness. The moral model (tracing back to the views shown in the Old and New Testaments) views blindness as something to be ashamed of and blind people as inferior. Some of the common stereotypes of blind people that fit with this idea are that blind people have many disabilities (as when someone shouts at me or asks the sighted person next to me what I want). Another version of this stereotype is when people pay a blind person what to them is a high compliment by saying "I don't think of you as blind." This stereotype is also seen when people assume that blind people are "superior" in some way, such as being above being interested in sex or being "so brave." About twenty years ago there was a giant flap about providing *Playboy* in Braille (no pictures) as part of the National Library Service magazine collection. Interestingly, no magazine racier than *Ladies Home Journal* is provided in Braille for women. In the moral view of blindness, a good blind person would be passive and grateful for charity shown.

The second concept of blindness is the medical model. What can't be fixed by modern medicine can be ameliorated by rehabilitation and education. Blind people can learn to read Braille, travel independently with white canes or guide dogs, and use talking computers. "Good" blind people in this paradigm seek to be cured of their blindness and if this is not possible to learn to exist as effectively as possible in a sighted world.

The third model of blindness treats blind people as a minority group. The last thirty-five years have seen "the last civil rights movement" happen when people with disabilities have banded together. This view sees a disability as the social, political, and cultural phenomenon that happens when a person has an impairment. To be considered a minority group, a group must meet certain criteria:

- the people in the group suffer prejudice and discrimination;
- people don't join the group by choice;
- they identify themselves as a group and usually intermarry.

Are people with disabilities a minority group? Through my writing about living with disabilities, I am saying that others share some of my experiences with disabilities and that we're a minority group. True, people cannot pick us out of a crowd as they can with some other minority groups. Sociologists, anthropologists, and other pundits may argue about whether or not we're a co-culture or a minority group. I can tell people firsthand what it feels like to be in the majority sometimes and then suddenly to be in the minority.

The minority group feeling of being an outsider is partially determined by whether or not my disability shows. It usually doesn't come into the conversation that I am blind and have fibromyalgia when I am talking to a stranger on the phone. Sometimes it suddenly comes out and then I am in a new category for that person. For example, one day the Water Department called to say that I'd filled out the water meter card wrong and asked if I would run down and read it again for them. I unthinkingly said, "No." When there was a moment of silence at the other end, I thought to add, "I'm blind and can't, so would you just estimate it?"

Occasionally, being blind is more of an issue, like the time I was talking to a nurse at the clinic about whether or not I needed to have a head bump checked out. She asked about my pupil sizes and I casually said, "Oh, I'm blind."

"You're what?" she questioned, with her voice about an octave higher than before. She thought that I meant I was blind from the head injury. In my slightly befuddled state I didn't think to explain that I'd been blind from birth.

Considering the reaction people often have to disabilities, it's

no wonder that people with invisible disabilities do not want to identify themselves as having a disability. I've known several friends who
have resisted getting glasses, hearing aids, or handicapped parking
stickers because they would rather be more limited than be labeled
handicapped. Clearly, our minority group often does not have a lot of
pride. Deaf pride, including the takeover of Gallaudet University
until a deaf president was found, is a wonderful counterexample. A
march in New York City by many disability groups to celebrate five
years of the Americans with Disabilities Act is another good start on
disability pride.

Whether a person will identify themselves as having a disability depends on how the question is asked. If they're asked, "Do
you have a disability that prevents you from doing your job?" very
few people would self-identify themselves as disabled. If the question was asked, "Do you have a disability or condition that changes
the way you do your job?" and examples were given, I'll bet more
people would identify themselves.

One might believe that determining the number of people
belonging to this minority group matters only to statisticians. However, consider that laws are made and services are funded based on
estimates of how much it will cost and how many will benefit. For
example, how many handicapped parking spaces should there be in
a parking lot with a hundred spaces? To answer that, it would be useful to know how many mobility-impaired people and people with
heart conditions, who need to limit walking, there are. If people are
afraid to be seen as different or handicapped, we'll never know.

In addition to whether I'm seen as disabled, part of feeling
like I'm part of a minority group comes from what we are doing. If
I'm at the Seeing Eye school training with a new dog, I'm no more
disabled than any other student. In the evening, after training is over,
there are many discussions of blindness and jokes told about us and
sighted people. For example, how about the time a guide dog (probably a retriever) paraded its owner proudly into the formal dining
room of the school with a bra hanging out of its grinning mouth? On
the other hand, if I'm sitting around with a bunch of sighted women
discussing which movie star looks the hottest or how to wash windows so they don't streak, suddenly I'm in the minority with little to
add.

Another part of being in a minority group that is certainly true for those of us with disabilities is that we are discriminated against. Two-thirds of working-aged people with disabilities who could work are unemployed. For instance, when the person who helps me vote has to sign on the back of my ballot (as is the law in Wisconsin), that's discrimination. One does not have to be a radical to want laws and attitudes to change. Needless to say, groups of people who are blind or have other disabilities have gotten together to lobby for legal and societal changes. My one and only experience bartending was at such a group's convention. The ethos that prevailed there was that just because I had never bartended was no reason I couldn't. I just asked people what they wanted in their martini, for example, and guessed at the amounts. There were no complaints, and that makes me wonder whether I was overestimating the required amount of liquor.

Unlike many minority groups, most people with disabilities do not have children with disabilities. Some disabilities are genetic, but the vast majority are not. They are also not contagious. I remember one woman getting her child out of a condo pool as soon as I got in, telling the child that she didn't want her to catch blindness. I swam several extra laps that day to deal with my anger.

Because disabilities are not usually inherited, it's important for adults with them to pass on "tricks of the trade" and ways of dealing with the nondisabled to kids with disabilities. When I got to play hostess to two young blind women (with their mothers and a teacher) to show them the wonders of going to the university where I work, I also brought them to my house to give them lunch and show them a blind woman living independently.

One of the mother's main questions was, "How do you know how much toothpaste is on your brush?"

"By touching it very lightly," I reassured her.

I was ready to talk about the big issues of her daughter's career and life goals, but she wanted to know first that her daughter wasn't going to go around the world with Crest from ear to ear. The daughter, on the other hand, was more interested in chatting up the blind male college student I'd asked to join us for lunch.

As with any minority group, there are subgroups that do not always agree or have the same needs. Partially sighted people may want print enlargement on their computers; I as a blind person want speech output. Dog users want rest stops for their guide dogs in airports for those long plane trips; cane users want to keep their canes by their seats on flights so they can move around the cabin. When minority groups start to fight about which is best, whose needs are the greatest, or who has been most victimized, everybody loses.

However, a bowling league I was on was a good example of intergroup cooperation. The league had about twenty-four bowlers, six of us with partial or total visual loss. We bowled right after a league of deaf people; it was quite a contrast between our noisiness and their quiet gabbing in sign language. Some of the visually impaired bowlers had tunnel vision so they could see down the alley and point out to us totally blind bowlers those nasty splits we had. But when it came time to go home, their cane use wasn't necessarily as good as some of the totally blind cane users. Both on and off the lanes, there was a spirit of good-natured kidding that was a good stress reliever for all of us no matter what our visual acuity.

What do those of us with disabilities want? I'll go out on a limb and make a couple of generalizations:

- We want opportunities as nearly equal as possible for the pursuit of the good things in life like education, work, and recreation. These opportunities may cost more to provide than for the nondisabled, but I don't think dollars and cents are all that should go into cost: benefit ratios.

- We want to be included in the mainstream of American life. Offer us help and ask for our help. If car rallies are your thing, could your club do a rally like the Braille Institute of America does in California where navigators are blind youths with Braille maps? If you're looking for new members for your women's group at church, don't hesitate to ask women with disabilities for fear that it would be too much trouble for them to host a meeting. Figure out together whether modifications should be made in the way hosting is done. Minorities plus majority equals everybody. We all have richer experiences that way.

Help That Helps: What Helping Professionals Should Do

The helping professions, as we call ourselves, have a lot to offer people, both with and without disabilities. However, I'm convinced we can unwittingly do immense harm as well. A couple of snapshots:

When I was in college I saw a counselor because of depression, family issues, and the usual mélange of late adolescent angst. One day my session ended late. The counselor advising me offered to walk across campus with me, taking some short cuts I did not know. I got to my class on time. I was personally struggling with issues of asking for and taking help. Having the help offered was a wonderful experience and I remember it thirty-five years later. Nowadays, in a time of skyrocketing malpractice claims, I don't know if that situation could happen again. His concrete action said more to me than a lot of discussion about whether it's okay to ask for help. A male counselor would probably be advised not to walk across campus with a female student, but was help that helped and did not demean.

On the other hand when I go to professional conventions in faraway cities, I often have trouble getting from place to place quickly in unfamiliar surroundings. I can count on one hand the number of offers I've received from fellow psychologists to accompany me even when we're going to the same place. In contrast, strangers and hotel personnel are often more helpful. I've asked a few of my colleagues why this happens. They usually say "I didn't want to demean you by offering help." It saddens me to think that people in the helping professions think it is demeaning to offer help. I don't believe the world is divided quite so neatly into helpers and helpees; I believe we are all *both* at times.

So what should you do to be helpful? First of all, when in doubt, offer help. The person with a disability can always say, "No thanks." You don't have to know what to do; saying, "May I help," lets me know you are there and are willing to help. Then I can direct you as to what I want. Then take the person's request seriously. If I say, "Let me take your left elbow to walk down the hall," don't grab my arm and push me ahead of you in a lawnmower approach.

If you're willing to be in an ongoing helping relationship with me, it's okay to talk with me about my disability and get your questions answered. You may need to ask what would be the most convenient way for me to fill out paperwork. If it is a sensitive question, please use discretion. For example, shouting my answers across the waiting room to the receptionist will probably not be my top choice. People have moved away from me when the veterinarian's receptionist shouted questions across the waiting room about my dog's diarrhea.

Taking me seriously as a client or parishioner also means trying to understand my lifestyle. Saying it's okay for me to read at Mass from my Braille scriptures, but asking me to leave my dog in the pew and have someone else lead me to the lectern, misses the point. I consider my Seeing Eye dog a gift from God and part of my life. This may mean dealing with your own discomfort about my blindness and visible brokenness. If you do this it may help you deal with many situations, including your own visible or invisible disabilities.

It's okay to be honest about your discomfort in helping a person with a disability. It may be a new experience, and sharing the discomfort openly can bring you and that person closer together. If you don't deal with the discomfort, it may take on a life of its own. I remember a supervisor who said at the end of a year of monitoring my work that his only feedback was that I should get dark glasses. His discomfort with my eyes had blocked out his ability to perceive anything I had done right or wrong in a year's worth of counseling.

When people ask questions and deal openly with their discomfort, the disability often fades into the background. It just becomes one part of who we are together.

Unfinished Business: Equality Is More Than Laws

Thirty years of legislation has done a lot to ensure that those of us with disabilities have access to education, public facilities, and employment, but I don't believe laws can change hearts and minds. That kind of change takes contact, good will, and a lot of discussion.

Sometimes in these discussions, it's difficult to know what words to use. Once I had a teacher who started to say "Seen any good movies lately?" and ended up with "S—Had contact with any good movies lately?" What is the politically correct term for someone who is blind or uses a wheelchair? When I moved to Eau Claire, the public library had a volunteer service that would deliver books to people who couldn't get to the library themselves or pick out their own books. At that time the service was called "Homebound." It is a wonderful service and I felt like a curmudgeon making a complaint, but the title Homebound made me imagine people tied to their front porch railings. After some lobbying, the library renamed the service Home Delivery.

In my opinion, the best word to use for describing a disability is the most accurate one. A person who has some vision is visually impaired. I am blind, not visually challenged or impaired; I do not see at all. People who use wheelchairs are wheelchair users—very few are wheelchair-bound. Schools for the blind are just that, they are not blind schools. Dogs that guide are guide dogs, not blind dogs. If the dog were truly a blind dog, then *it* would need a guide dog.

Unfortunately, our language includes many slams connected with disability words. When people say, "What are you, blind or something?" when they mean "stupid," that is offensive. Blind fool, blind fate, and blind rage are just a few slams connected with blindness. The only possibly positive phrase connected with blindness is "blind pig" —a place to get liquor during Prohibition. I understand what you mean even if I don't "see" what you mean. If you were to say "Seen any good movies lately?" it wouldn't bother me nearly as much as stumbling around trying to be extra sensitive. If you're a good friend, and I'm feeling feisty, I may tease you about your sightist language and you may get away with calling me a blind fool.

Beyond which words to use, developing a mentality focused on how can we work around our differences and still enjoy them goes a long way. Even if you don't know exactly what to do with a particular person with a disability, you can work it out together. I think fear often gets in the way: fear of offending, fear of doing the wrong thing, or fear of looking stupid. When I first spent time with people who were wheelchair users, the same fears hit me. How would we walk together? How could I talk face to face with them without spending my life kneeling? Mucking through these differences led to some fun and treasured memories.

One evening, I invited a couple over for chili; the man was blind and his wife was a wheelchair user. I am a vegetarian; however, they felt strongly that their chili should have meat. Reluctantly, I agreed to fry the hamburger and add it to their chili. After they arrived, I threw the hamburger in a frying pan and went to visit the restroom. Beth, my Seeing Eye dog, smelled the meat cooking (an unusual event in a vegetarian household) and decided to take advantage of some before it got too hot to snatch. As I heard her front feet leave the floor, I came running out of the bathroom with my pants around my ankles. The woman in the wheelchair sat at the kitchen door transfixed, but unable to do anything because the door was too narrow for her wheelchair to fit through. Fortunately, her husband couldn't see me hobbling across the kitchen with my pants down, trying to get Beth away from the pan before she got burned or reached the hamburger. When it all ended, the chili tasted fine (both meaty and meatless) and the evening was enjoyed with a good laugh among good friends.

A level playing field is important. If we're going to play cards or Scrabble™, it has to be with my Braille set; if I bowl with you, you'll need to tell me which pins I knocked down. At my goddaughter's birthday party (she has cerebral palsy and used a walker at that time) they played musical spots instead of musical chairs. Once at work, my boss kept suggesting that the staff play Frisbee to help us bond. I was hurt and angry, but wasn't quick enough to say "Sure, let's play at midnight in the woods."

If you and I are making brownies for the Humane Society sale, it will work best if we specialize. I bake and you frost; you cut and I bag. And of course, my guide dog is in charge of supervision and floor cleaning afterwards.

As any parent of two or more children knows, treating equally does not always mean treating the same. If I walk into a restaurant and am handed a non-Braille menu, I've been treated the same as any other customer, but not equally. If the server asks me "What do you want?" instead of going through the menu with me, it's not equal. How do I know what I want until I know what they have? Or if the Braille menu, in those few wonderful places that do have them, does not have prices on it, that's a problem for me. Of course, the "treat equally, not the same" obligation applies to me too. If a server spends time going through the menu with me, I tip more.

If the accommodations are there, those of us with disabilities will be out there working, playing, loving, and praying with those without disabilities. I believe that the acceptance, tolerance, and embracing of differences will occur.

Pearls: The Positives of Having Disabilities

When an oyster makes a pearl, it's out of a grain of sand that's irritating it. Without the irritant, there is no pearl. I would bet if you interviewed the oyster during the process, it would not wish for the grain of sand to be there. Even worse, after the oyster makes the pearl, it may lose it to some human.

At least we get to keep the pearls we've developed from living with disabilities and illnesses. Would I rather be able to see? Yes and no. Dr. Oliver Sachs, a noted neurologist, did a case study on a man who was blind and got his sight back, but went blind again and was more content that way. It may sound crazy to those of you who can see, but I can understand it. If I could see, I'd lose part of who I am. For example, if I could see my guide dog, I couldn't have her. Hence I'd go to work or church alone. My dogs are so much more than a cane with four legs and a tail. Watching my dog's reactions to people, and those of people to him or her, makes ordinary events fun. A toddler grinning from ear to ear yelling, "Dog, dog!" brightened up a recent shopping trip. I also wouldn't have to take my dog outdoors when it's twenty below zero during winter in Wisconsin, but that's a small price to pay for the good times we share.

Then there are the good things I've learned about human nature because I'm blind. The only way I can tell a one-dollar from a five-dollar bill is by asking. So far, I've only been cheated once. A good testimony to people's honesty, I'd say! Or, take all the times perfect strangers have helped me get where I'm going. I remember one time I was trying to get from one part of Alexandria, Louisiana, to the opposite side of the town. Buses were not running, and I didn't know where to find a phone to call a cab. Finally I just stuck out my thumb. Lots of cars went by, but one eventually stopped. My guide dog and I jumped in and I asked if we could have a ride back to Central Louisiana State Hospital where I was interning. The driver said "Sure." As we proceeded, he commented that not too many white women would take a ride from an unfamiliar Black man. I assured him that I didn't care and appreciated his kindness.

One day I was crossing a busy street in Scranton, Pennsylvania, and a street person came up and began helping me. I didn't really need her help and started telling her so. She said, "I feel sorry for you not being able to see." I started to straighten her out—I had a doctorate, a good job, and a roof over my head. Luckily, before my mouth opened, it dawned on me that this was somebody feeling good about being able to help someone, and maybe she didn't have that opportunity often. I just said "thanks for the help."

Being blind has also helped to develop my patience. I am not a patient person yet, but I know I'm more patient than I would be if I could see. John Milton's sonnet about his blindness contains the line: "They also serve who only stand and wait." That still describes those of us with disabilities several hundred years after it was written. I spend a lot of time waiting. I wait to receive books on tape from a library across the state; they send something from a list I've sent in months ago. I wait until I have a reader to read a nice juicy personal letter, unless the sender has typed it so I can read it on my reading machine or has emailed it to me. I wait for a neighbor to come home and run over to my house, only to find out that a note taped to the door is offering to edge my sidewalks, not telling me that I've won the lottery. Luckily, I have a dog who likes to take many long walks; and walking helps calm me down and make me more patient.

There's also the pearl of satisfaction that comes with life's small accomplishments. When I make a batch of muffins, it's sort of a messy procedure. I have to touch the papers to know where to put the batter. The muffins may end up with little blobs of batter on the outside of the cups. They may not look like something for the front cover of *Better Homes and Gardens,* but they still taste great.

Once I had a troop of Girl Scouts and their leaders at my house for a disability awareness seminar. The girls wanted to experience blindness, so we made cookies in the dark. After twelve people, supervised by a Labrador under the table, got done making cookies and bumping into each other in a fairly small kitchen, one girl commented, "These are the best cookies I've ever had in my life." Here's the recipe:

2 cups peanut butter

2 cups sugar

2 eggs

1/2 cup flour

Mix ingredients and then bake on an ungreased cookie sheet at 350 degrees for about twelve minutes or until they smell done. You'd better try it in the dark to really have them taste super!

I'm also aware of the interdependence we all share, more than I would be if I could see. My brother commented on this once, envying the number of friends I have no matter where I've lived. "You always seem to find good people," he said, and I agreed that it was true. People know I need them. I give back what I can, and friendships often follow. I'll bet if I could be more independent I would not have developed the friendliness I have, and my world would be much poorer.

Last, but not least, is the pearl of humor. In so many situations in my life I could have either laughed or cried. Finding the humor in these situations has brought me through. One time I closed a talk by saying, "if you want to ask a question you don't have to raise your hand, because I won't see it and your arm will get tired." The audience erupted in laughter. It turned out that the town's mayor already had his hand up to pose a question. He was able to laugh, too, about old habits dying hard.

To determine if a pearl is genuine, one bites it. If it's gritty, it's a real pearl. The same holds true with the metaphorical pearls one finds in disabilities or other life situations. One still tastes the grit in the situation.

Second Adulthood with Disabilities: What Are You Going to Do With the Rest of Your Life?

When you cease to make a contribution,
you begin to die.

—Eleanor Roosevelt

From what we get we can make a living.
What we give, however, makes a life.

—Arthur Ashe

Gail Sheehy writes about second adulthood: the time of life after about age forty-five. I'm among the 76 million baby boomers that are making choices about working/retiring and how we want to write the rest of the story of our lives. For me, turning fifty-four and realizing that by the law of averages about two thirds of my time on earth was gone put these questions into sharper focus.

Arranging for my dad's care as he became ill and died and providing respite care for a friend with Alzheimer's educated me about the struggles faced by the fifteen million Americans who daily take care of their aged or severely ill or disabled relatives. In my dad's last few months, this became a two- or three-hour daily time commitment for me, making arrangements, finding resources, and talking to him and caregivers about his daily needs. Since he lived in Arizona and I live in Wisconsin, the phone company benefited greatly. His discomfort with my disabilities and the fact that it would take time for me to develop a support system in his town so I could operate independently there dissuaded me from taking leave at work and managing the caregiving on site. A few times when I went out I scrounged around his cupboards, not knowing what the canned goods were. I figured out it was just easier to fill my knapsack with food when I came out, so I knew what I was cooking and serving. It amazes me that for the most part, hospital staffs and in-home care-givers have had no training in assisting a blind person.

As our population ages (the rate of blindness in the sixty-five-plus age group is twice that of those under sixty-five), there will be need for a lot of in-services about quick and dirty methods to help especially newly blind people be as independent as possible. For example, if you can't see, how do you mark pill bottles if you can't read Braille? I suggest the rubber band method; put as many rubber bands around the bottle as times per day that you have to take the pill. Some people like the pill boxes with a little door for each day, but that one takes someone filling it for the person if they don't know which bottle is which.

Since you're not getting continuing education units for your how-to-treat-your-aging-and-newly-blind-relative lesson, I'll just give you a piece of doggerel to consider:

Let me take your arm; don't push me from behind.

Don't point; describe the situation, to get it in my mind.

Don't move my stuff without telling me, I ask

And help, don't do it for me, if it is my task.

Be patient as I adjust and learn to do things on my own

Remember, you don't have to fix it; you can just listen to me moan.

I appreciate the help, when you can freely give

But when you can't, tell me. We'll both still love and live.

In providing respite care for my neighbor with Alzheimer's, I've learned some lessons that I'm sure will be useful for my second adulthood. The first is that during this part of life, it may help to switch to the Buddhist Olympics perspective: the last one over the finish line wins. One day, this neighbor and I took a day trip to a friend's farm. Our trip accomplished nothing in the sense of getting her garden weeded and wasn't remembered a day later, but the sights, sounds, smells, and tastes were enjoyed moment by moment.

Aging is funny business. Other muscles may sag but laugh muscles will get plenty of use if you let them. A trip to see where my Seeing Eye dog was going to retire, with my Alzheimer's friend in tow, was misperceived as a failure. My friend thought he was supposed to supervise the dog procreating with the "girlfriend," (the family's German shepherd), not just enjoying a romp. The procreating would have been a true miracle since both dogs are fixed.

As I watch church members and friends pitch in to take this man with Alzheimer's on outings and give his wife time to accomplish tasks uninterrupted, I'm reminded that "it takes a village." This time it's to care for our elders instead of raising our children.

I am watching friends my age move to houses on one level, especially those who have broken a leg. I helped clean out my dad's house and became convinced to lighten my load. Do I need notes that I taught from years ago? When I lost five thousand emails I'd saved with one wrong keystroke, I realized maybe this was a blessing. The jokes among them will recycle in a year or so anyway. A friend came and helped me sort out nine bags of clothes for Goodwill. Gravity has changed my shape in the ten years since we last did this. We discovered some real finds: almost as good as a move, but without all the boxing hassles!

I also notice my career focus changing to emphasize training, mentoring, and trying to make situations better for the next generation of psychologists. I do research with younger faculty and staff and take them to conventions to present our results. I enjoy watching them accomplish these professional milestones more than I enjoy doing them myself. I joined the Committee for Disability Issues in Psychology of the American Psychological Association to help my profession use the gifts of psychologists with disabilities. I've had the chance to coach a few young blind psychologists by email. They really like being able to ask the small questions of someone who has been there, like "How do you know when a session of fifty minutes' duration is over when you can't glance at a clock?" I point out that although opening a Braille watch is more noticeable than glancing at a clock, it does show the client that I am comfortable with my limits and will do what it takes to get the job done without apology for doing it differently. Email is wonderful because I can coach someone halfway around the world. It is sometimes hard to get the spirit of encouragement and empowerment into an email message, even though there are plenty of acronyms for emotional phrases like "LOL" ("laughing out loud" is the translation, by the way.)

With my inheritance from my dad, I started a small scholarship at my university for a student with a disability who is majoring in psychology. Less than 1% of American Psychological Association members report having a disability…a far cry from the one of seven Americans who have one. We're underrepresented and I need to do what I can to remedy this situation.

I'm really enjoying the freedom second adulthood brings to play "payback." Whether it's speaking to nurses about conflict management (after first pointing out that I wouldn't be around if it weren't for good nurses when I was born) or starting awards for children's book authors who write good books with disabled characters in them, I'm able to nurture parts of the world that nurtured me. I feel like a grandma to the world. I've visited several former student readers who are twenty-something now and it's great to see how they are getting on with their lives. I can encourage them, enjoy them, and give them back their babies when they cry!

My sense of time seems to be changing in some ways too. People often ask: "what do you do all day?" assuming that blind people don't work, volunteer, watch television, waste time on computer games, etc. like sighted people. Unfortunately, I stand convicted of doing all the above except the television addiction and have neatly substituted reading and listening to public radio for that. Empty time is not the issue. Having time enough to accomplish what I want to and at the same time wanting to take more time to smell the roses pulls me in two directions. Hurry up so you can slow down and enjoy life—that's the treadmill I'm on in my second adulthood.

Hoping to change this, I went with a friend to a local group meeting of the Red Hat Society. The newest member of Here Come the Red Hats! Here Come the Red Hats! of Eau Claire came to her first meeting dressed in red and purple of course, but also in black fur and a pink scarf. My Seeing Eye dog, Garlyn, was only two and a half; a pink scarf contrasted well with her black shiny fur coat. We're all familiar with the statistics about increasing rates of various illnesses and disabilities as we age, but the Red Hat spirit of enjoying life, having fun, and making friends is powerful medicine for healing the isolation that often comes with illnesses and disabilities. With no prompting, but with a positive example set by Queen Bonnie, Garlyn and I were embraced by a chapter of dog-lovers, cancer survivors, hip- and knee-replacement owners, and others who clearly knew that it's the spirit, not the perfect health status, that matters in the world of Red Hats.

I also notice an increasing interest in religion/spirituality, apparently shared by many baby boomers. *The Big Bang, Buddha and the Baby Boom,* and *Goddesses in Older Women* are just two of the latest offerings in this genre. Maybe the blind soothsayer in Oedipus Rex will be my next archetypal model.

I've got one piece of advice for you baby boomers who are developing disabilities: try looking at the chronic illness or disability as the destination of a trip, sort of like going to Rome. You know how to research destinations and sort through all the information to figure out how you want to explore the destination. Reading this memoir and checking out organizations like those listed in the reference section can help you begin the journey planning for Destination Disability.

Are We There Yet? Final Thoughts and a Quiz

Have we reached the point where people with disabilities can work, play, love, and pray along with people without disabilities? I think we're going in the right direction, but we're not there yet.

In the area of employment, seventy percent of people with disabilities of working age are still unemployed; obviously there's a long way to go until we reach equality in employment. There are positive signs like McJobs, a McDonald's program for hiring people with cognitive disabilities, and laws like the Americans with Disabilities Act.

As the average age of Americans rises and people retire later, it only makes good business sense to accommodate employees' disabilities. Even though most disabled people who are unemployed would rather work than take government money, the Social Security Disability Income needs to continue until the employment picture becomes more positive.

The people at work make all the difference between a happily employed person with a disability and one who just puts in hours for a paycheck. Recently I was to receive an award from my employer and asked one of the administrators to help me practice the award ceremony beforehand. (I wanted to be sure that my dog and my six feet were going to the right place at the right time.) The administrator told me it was "easy" and that I didn't need to practice. I restated my request and he restated that it was easy! The discussion was particularly ironic because part of the reason I was receiving the award was for my work in the area of disability awareness. The ending was happy: he agreed, we practiced, and when the big day came the ceremony went fine.

We've gone beyond having the first disabled superstars, like a former Miss America who is deaf, but we have not reached the point where a person with a disability evokes no more comment than one without. Unfortunately, going from tokenism to full integration may take generations.

Disabled people helping each other has become more common. Magazines for parents of blind children written by blind adults can help parents realize the realities of living as a blind person in a sighted world. Articles for blind teens written by blind adults highlighting ordinary people (who happen to be blind) doing ordinary things are good efforts. Historically, deaf people have been far ahead of any other disability group in passing on their "culture" to the next generation. Support groups for people with a particular illness or disability run by people with that disability can also build the self-esteem and survival skills it takes to achieve a full life.

Unfortunately, some people are only partially aware of how to interact helpfully with people with disabilities. On a recent stroll through the woods with my guide dog, I met a runner. The runner said, "There's a tree down so you can hardly get through," and then ran off. "Where?" I wanted to bellow after her, but it was too late. I'm sure her intentions were good, but she did not give me enough information to be helpful. If men are from Mars and women are from Venus, maybe we need communication workshops like "Blind People are From Pluto and Sighted People are From Saturn."

Now that you've read the book, it's time for a five-question mastery quiz! See how you scored below.

1. You find out your blind date is blind. You should:
   A. Get rid of your movie tickets and plan to play blind man's bluff.
   B. Check to make sure the movie does not have subtitles only.
   C. Call off the date because "Aunt Ethel died." You've never met a blind person and it would make you nervous.

2. You see someone getting out of a car parked in a *handicapped* spot who looks okay to you. You should:
   A. Ask to see their doctor's note.

B. Assume that they may have a hidden condition like heart disease or fibromyalgia.

C. Break their leg so they'll really need the spot next time.

3. Your boss has hearing loss and you want a raise. You should:

A. Shout at her to make sure she hears your request.

B. Face her and talk clearly without putting your hand in front of your mouth.

C. Go to her boss, because you don't feel comfortable with her.

4. When talking with someone in a wheelchair you should:

A. Shout, because they probably can't hear either.

B. Sit at their level if possible.

C. Talk to their nondisabled friend, but be nice and ask about them.

5. You notice my Seeing Eye dog is getting gray. You should:

A. Ask me how long guide dogs live, and get all the facts you can.

B. Say nothing if you're just an acquaintance, but if you're a good friend ask me how things are going.

C. Anonymously give me some doggie Grecian® Formula™.

Scoring: If you answered "B" to all of the questions, you are a certified, sensitive, wonderful human being, especially if you paid for this book rather than skimming through it at the bookstore. If you answered anything other than B, the good news is you can still improve. You can either read this book again, or wait until the movie comes out and catch it with a blind date!

Author's Notes

This book has been ten years in the making and numerous people have contributed to it by their encouragement, advice, and patience with me and my laborious writing process. Lynne Warnke retyped the first few chapters back when I was using a manual typewriter and she had an electric one. Terri, Tina, Julie, Katie, Karin, and other readers: hard to believe it, isn't it—it's finally in print! A special thanks to Doc Reed and others who kept asking when it would be published and where could they buy a copy. Buy now, Doc, and I'll autograph for free!

Dr. Ruth Cronje and two of her editing classes at the University of Wisconsin-Eau Claire deserve special mention. As part of their class, these students combed through the manuscript letter by letter and comma by comma and then had to justify their edits to me as well as to their teacher. I learned a lot from them and will never forget the difference between an "m-dash" and an "n-dash." Thanks particularly to Becca Hutchinson, who did a final edit, and to Dr. Cronje for all her work on this manuscript. I can't imagine a more enthusiastic, hard-working, and competent editor.

Small portions of this manuscript have been published in the Eau Claire *Leader/Telegram, America Magazine, Wilderlust,* edited by Chrissy Laws, and *The Red Hat Society's® Laugh Lines,* by Sue Ellen Cooper.

Last, but certainly not least, thanks go to Sugar, Tatum, Carter, and Garlyn, my Seeing Eye dogs who lived through my writing. Sometimes they missed out on a walk or play period because The Author was at work and sometimes they got an extra walk because The Author needed to manage her authorial stress. They took it in relatively good humor, as part of a dog's life catering to a cranky human. Without them and their predecessors, my adventures in living with disabilities wouldn't have been nearly as much fun.

References and Recommended Reading

Cooper, S.E. (2005). The Red Hat Society's® *Laugh Lines: Stories of Inspiration and Hattitude,* New York: Warner.

Erin, J. (1991). Religious beliefs of parents with children with visual impairments. *Journal of Visual Impairment and Blindness, 85,* 157–162.

Hine, R. (1994). *Second Sight.* Thorndike, ME: Thorndike.

Hull, J. (1991). *Touching the Rock.* New York: Random House.

Johnson, B. (1992). Splashes of Joy in the Cesspool of Life. Dallas, TX: Word Publications.

Laws, C. (Ed.) (2004). *Wilderlust.* Bradford, ME: NHEST.

Mairs, N. (1994). *Voice Lessons: On Becoming a (Woman) Writer.* Boston, MA: Beacon Press.

Milian, M. & Erin, J. (eds.) (2001). *Diversity and Visual Impairment.* New York: AFB Press.

Sacks, O. (1995). *An Anthropologist on Mars.* New York: Knopf.

Shawcross, J.T. (ed.) (1971). *The Collected Poetry of John Milton.* Garden City, NY: Doubleday.

Tada, J.E. (2001). *Ordinary People, Extraordinary Faith: Stories of Inspiration.* Nashville, TN: Thomas Nelson.

Organizations

American Council of the Blind (ACB)
1155 15th Street NW, Suite 720
Washington, DC 20005
(202) 467–5081
(800) 424–8666
www.acb.org

ACB is an information, referral, and advocacy organization with 52 state/regional affiliates. The goals of ACB are to improve the well-being of people who are blind or visually impaired through legislative advocacy, to encourage persons who are blind or have visual impairments to develop their abilities, and to promote a greater understanding of people who are blind or have visual impairments. ACB also has a student chapter, National Alliance of Blind Students (NABS).

American Foundation for the Blind (AFB)
11 Penn Plaza, Suite 300
New York, NY 10011
(212) 502–7600
(800) 232–5463
afbinfo@afb.net
www.afb.org

AFB provides information and consultation in the areas of education, rehabilitation, employment, and special products. It also publishes *The Journal of Visual Impairment and Blindness*, and *AccessWorld®*. AFB also has a career database and an adaptive technology database. Six regional centers around the country provide advice, technical assistance, and referral to local services and agencies.

John Milton Society for the Blind (JMS)

www.jmsblind.org

JMS provides referrals for religious materials in alternate formats.

National Federation of the Blind (NFB)

1800 Johnson Street

Baltimore, MD 21230

(410) 659–9314

www.nib.org

NFB is a consumer group that can answer questions about blindness, refer people to appropriate resources or adapted equipment, and send a publications list. NFB has a number of scholarships available for students in postsecondary education. It also publishes *The Braille Monitor*, and sponsors JOB (Job Opportunities for the Blind), a job listing and referral service.

National Library Service for the Blind and Physically Handicapped (NLS)

www.loc.gov/nls

NLS provides books in Braille and on tape from regional libraries in each state, and has reference materials and bibliographies on many subjects, including religious materials in alternate formats.

Recording for the Blind and Dyslexic (RFB & D)

20 Roszel Road

Princeton, NJ 08540

(609) 452–0606

(800) 221–4972 (book orders only)

www.rfbd.org

RFB & D is a nonprofit service organization providing recorded textbooks, electronic books, library services, and other educational services to individuals who can't read regular print because of a visual, perceptual, or physical disability. RFB&D registration requires documentation of disability, an initial registration fee of $65, and an annual fee of $35. Institutional registration costs $350–$950, depending on how many books the college or university borrows.

Seeing Eye, Inc.™

Box 375

Morristown, NJ 07963-0375

www.seeingeye.org

The Seeing Eye is the oldest guide dog school in North America, providing trained guide dogs to qualified blind and visually impaired adults.

Printed in the United States
60542LVS00003B/175

9 781598 581317